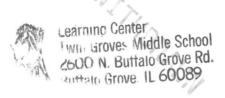

**FAMOUS
FASHION
DESIGNERS**

ISAAC MIZRAHI

FAMOUS FASHION DESIGNERS

COCO CHANEL

MARC JACOBS

CALVIN KLEIN

RALPH LAUREN

STELLA McCARTNEY

ISAAC MIZRAHI

VALENTINO

VERSACE

FAMOUS
FASHION
DESIGNERS

ISAAC MIZRAHI

Clifford W. Mills

CHELSEA HOUSE
An Infobase Learning Company

ISAAC MIZRAHI

Copyright © 2011 by Infobase Learning

Chelsea House
An imprint of Infobase Learning
132 West 31st Street
New York NY 10001

Library of Congress Cataloging-in-Publication Data

Mills, Cliff, 1947–
  Isaac Mizrahi / by Clifford W. Mills.
    p. cm. — (Famous fashion designers)
  Includes bibliographical references and index.
  ISBN 978-1-60413-984-6 (hardcover)
  1. Mizrahi, Isaac—Juvenile literature. 2. Fashion designers—United States—Biography—Juvenile literature. 3. Fashion designers—New York (State)—New York—Biography—Juvenile literature. I. Mizrahi, Isaac. II. Title.
  TT505.M595M55 2011
  746.9'2092—dc22
  [B]   2010033973

Chelsea House books are available at special discounts when purchased in bulk quantities for businesses, associations, institutions, or sales promotions. Please call our Special Sales Department in New York at (212) 967-8800 or (800) 322-8755.

You can find Chelsea House on the World Wide Web at
http://www.chelseahouse.com

Text design by Lina Farinella
Composition by EJB Publishing Services
Cover design by Alicia Post
Cover printed by Bang Printing, Brainerd, Minn.
Book printed and bound by Bang Printing, Brainerd, Minn.
Date printed: January 2011
Printed in the United States of America

10 9 8 7 6 5 4 3 2 1

Contents

1

Unzipped

Some of America's most dazzling theater is found not only on New York City's neon-lit Broadway but blocks away in an area known as the Garment District. The showrooms, lofts, museums, school auditoriums, and other spaces in the Garment District often have as much magic in the air as Broadway, even if they don't have marquee lights. Many of the most famous fashion designers in the world have offices in and around the avenue, where they design, produce, and show garments that are often called "wearable art."

The theater for their most dramatic wearable art performances was a group of tents in the Garment District's backyard, Bryant Park. Twice a year from 1993 to 2010, this area behind the New York Public Library staged the designers' fall and spring fashion seasons' collections during New York Fashion Week. [The event has since moved to Lincoln Center.] Buyers, celebrities, and the media are usually the main audience for each fashion show. But many more people want to see, feel, and hear the beauty, sheer drama, and pulsing music that surround young, beautiful models in eye-catching apparel as they walk down a long, narrow stage called a runway.

The entrance to the main tent at Bryant Park displayed many quotations from designers and fashion journalists, one of which was from *Vogue* magazine editor Anna Wintour: "Bryant Park became the beacon of what New York fashion stands for—an industry that's fearless, tireless, and always moving forward." One of fashion's guiding lights is also fearless, tireless, and always moving forward. His name is Isaac Mizrahi.

PLANNING FOR AN EVENING TO REMEMBER

On Tuesday evening, April 12, 1994, Mizrahi made fashion history when he showed his fall collection. He was being filmed by a movie team. The director, Douglas Keeve, wanted to capture not just one designer but an entire industry in what became the documentary film *Unzipped*.

Mizrahi's previous show, of his spring 1994 collection, had received bad reviews. Since he was a "hot" designer, much was expected of each show and garment. When he read that he didn't impress the audience with his last show and that his famous sense of color, shape, and fabric had failed him, he felt terrible. And he knew that he was under extra pressure with his April 12 performance.

Like all fashion shows, his fall collection originated with a single idea. Mizrahi had been watching a movie, *The Call of the Wild*. One scene set in a wild and frozen northern forest depicts the hero, played by Clark Gable, rescuing his heroine, played by Loretta Young. Even though she was nearly frozen to death, she looked beautiful wrapped in fur, with her makeup and lip gloss perfectly in place (Hollywood is, after all, a dream factory), causing Mizrahi to remark to the cameras following him everywhere, "If you must freeze on the tundra, this is the way to do it."

The image of the actress in that scene set Mizrahi's imagination and creativity into action. He began to make hundreds of sketches of jackets, coats, dresses, and boots that played on the idea of being protected by fur. Real fur in fashion had become unfashionable by the early 1990s, and animal rights activists made life very uncomfortable for those wrapped in the luxurious garments. A woman wanting to show her status and wealth with real fur might have blood or paint thrown on her. Fake fur was beginning to come into its own, and Mizrahi wanted to use that fact while still reminding people of the Inuit culture and drawing on a fashion statement that had been made since medieval times.

But fur alone was not enough to make a collection. Mizrahi has always been interested in vivid colors and combining them in unexpected ways to provoke certain emotions. He has also always been interested in combining "high" and "low" fashion, pairing the expensive with the inexpensive. In addition, he likes to combine clothes people wear during the day (day wear) with clothes they usually wear when out at night (evening wear). He was, he says in the movie, creating a look that could then create a show.

CASTING AND PRODUCING THE SHOW

The next step in creating the look for the April 1994 show was having pattern makers turn his sketches into patterns that could be shaped and made into one-of-a-kind samples. Muslin (a cloth) was fitted onto mannequins (replicas of the human form) and then live models. The garments were shaped and reshaped under Mizrahi's guidance. The whole process becomes, according to him, "a giant puzzle."

Mizrahi finally had the "plot" for his show. Now he needed to cast the characters. He assembled five of the most famous fashion models of all time: Naomi Campbell, Cindy Crawford, Linda Evangelista, Christy Turlington, and Kate Moss. He also cast several others for

Drawing inspiration from an old Hollywood movie, Mizrahi focused on creating a new look for his Fall 1994 collection by adding fur to his signature style of mixing "high" and "low" fashion. Top supermodels of the time, including Linda Evangelista (*above*), were featured in his show.

the show, including Carla Bruni, who would become the first lady of France in 2008 after marrying French president Nicolas Sarkozy.

After the plot and characters, Mizrahi needed to hire production consultants to create the set and lighting and to help decide on the music that would play during the show. Dressers for the models and hairstylists and makeup artists needed to be planned for as well. When the team fell into place and worked together for several weeks, the giant puzzle was finally almost finished. Large doses of both inspiration and perspiration were needed.

Goddesses of the Catwalk: The Runway Model

Few occupations are as glamorous as a female runway model for the fashion industry. Most are 5 feet 9 inches (175 centimeters) or taller, very thin (108 to 115 pounds, or 49 to 52 kilograms), and very young (15 to 22 years old). They are like the princesses in fairy tales, young and beautiful. And like Snow White's jealous stepmother, some want to be seen as the fairest in the land.

They strike poses for money, often a great deal of money. But they must get used to depriving themselves of food, constant travel with hours at a time in airports, demanding photographers and designers, and endless modeling sessions that can entail 50 or more clothing changes.

Isaac Mizrahi attracts and casts some of the most famous runway models. For his April 1994 show, he cast a team of superstars that he knew would portray his collection particularly well.

Naomi Campbell in 1994 was making millions of dollars a year. She had been discovered in the 1980s by designer Gianni Versace as a perfect vehicle for his colorful and provocative fashions. She was expressive, confident, and often called one of the goddesses of the catwalk (as the runway is also called). As an assertive black woman, she also helped change the face of fashion.

THE TENSION BUILDS

Just before the fashion show opened, Mizrahi was captured by the *Unzipped* cameras, which showed him to be clearly both excited and nervous. He said that he liked to be in control but felt out of control in the days and moments before the performance. He noted that a fashion show "has to be the most wonderful 20 minutes of a designer's life." But he knew how important this show was to his career. He had thrown his heart and soul into the look and the show. But how would the fashion world react?

Cindy Crawford had been an accomplished athlete and an A student in high school and by 1994 had been a finalist in Elite's Model Look Contest. She loved the camera and it loved her. She became the face of Revlon cosmetics, a television and movie actor, and a force in the housewares design business.

Linda Evangelista has been called one of the best runway models ever, and her career was taking off in the early 1990s. She cut her hair short and was magic on the runway with her smile and energy. She focused on her modeling and few other interests.

Christy Turlington started modeling at the age of 13 and soon won the Face of the Twentieth Century Award given by New York's Metropolitan Museum. She refused to give up her high school studies for modeling, saying many times that teenagers should always finish at least high school. One of the most socially conscious models, she refused to wear fur and worked with several organizations that try to identify injustices around the world.

The fifth of Mizrahi's supermodels was Kate Moss. She was discovered by a modeling agency when she was 14 and returning from a family vacation in the Bahamas. She soon was on the covers of the major fashion magazines—*Vogue, Elle,* and *Harper's Bazaar.* Unfortunately, like some runway models, her life spun out of control, and in 1998 she checked herself into the Priory Clinic in London to deal with depression and drug abuse. She got help, matured, and has now become an award-winning designer of handbags and other accessories.

The audience slowly filled in the many rows at the main Bryant Park tent. Actors Robert De Niro and Richard Gere sat on each side of the beginning of the catwalk. Liza Minnelli, Ellen Barkin, Roseanne Barr, and Sandra Bernhard were also among the celebrities waiting to see if Mizrahi could make a comeback. And security guards had their hands full keeping out people who were not on the invitation list.

The models, dressers, hairstylists, makeup artists, and Mizrahi himself were all separated from the audience by a thin curtain called a scrim. Depending on the lighting, the scrim could either be hard to see through or a veil that was transparent. It was either a wall or a window, depending on how the light struck it. This was groundbreaking for a fashion show. Mizrahi wanted the backstage area to be onstage, to be part of the show. It was a move that many models objected to but others welcomed. Mizrahi doesn't like to hide things—feelings, the process of creating, his models, anything. He loves to reveal.

The designer, in black slacks, a black sweater, and a white shirt, was everywhere backstage before the show, making last-second adjustments to models' hats and coats. Racks of clothes were everywhere. The models completed their makeup sessions, including several cries of pain during eyebrow tweezing. The tension built and showed on Mizrahi's expressive face.

LET THE SHOW BEGIN

Finally, when he said, "Go music," and "Let's go," the show was on. To the upbeat of "You Make Me Feel (Mighty Real)," Linda Evangelista lengthened her stride, came out from behind the scrim, and hit the runway. She was wearing a brown fake-fur hat, gray-green jacket and skirt, white blouse, and white fake-fur calf warmers. The flashbulbs popped, and many in the overflow audience craned their necks to see the stunning model.

Mizrahi suddenly stopped Kate Moss before she entered the runway and adjusted the collar of her coat. She was wearing pink

Fashion shows are meant to showcase the clothes in a designer's latest collection. Presented seasonally, these productions can help a designer make a splash among the fashion industry's elite and can generate business. *Above,* Mizrahi's Fall 1996 fashion show.

fake fur that looked like fleece or sheepskin. Her bright red lip gloss shone in the lights, and her hair was pulled back and twisted, but the designer needed to be an instant sculptor to get exactly

ELEMENTS OF STYLE

Before you can think about having style, you have to learn to look in the mirror and like what you see. . . . I can give you all my style tips and ideas about your hair, makeup, and dress, but none of this is going to do anything for you if you don't learn to accept yourself and love who you are. . . .

I will tell you that I work with plenty of different types [of people]: Some skinny, some average, some actually fat. . . . Children need to be told how beautiful they are again and again, until they finally believe it. . . .

That's what [style] . . . is about: Reinforcing everything about you that is already beautiful and reminding yourself so many times that eventually you believe you're beautiful without me or anyone else telling you so. It sounds too easy, but accentuating what's right about you is probably harder than remedying what's wrong. Try it and keep doing it. This is the best style advice I can give to anyone.

—*Isaac Mizrahi in* How to Have Style

the look he wanted. No detail was too small to overlook. Moss was then released onto the stage to flaunt her look.

As each model came back off the stage, she became a quick-change artist. With her dresser frantically pulling off one set of clothes and putting on another, she had no time to lose. Boots were the hardest things to change, and several models had to kick while lying on the floor in an effort to release their footwear.

Some of the models got into the pulsing of the music and swayed backstage in the moments before they made their next run. They got into a flow of energy and rhythm that seemed to spread to the audience looking in on them. Models and audience fed off each other.

One of Cindy Crawford's outfits was a pink skirt and top covered by a black fake-fur coat. She knew exactly when and how much of the coat to take off to reveal the clothes underneath. Naomi Campbell made an indelible impression in a vibrant brown jacket and skirt. The colors, shapes, and textures paraded up and down the runway.

When the last model returned backstage, Mizrahi put his head in his hands in relief and exhaustion. Then, after 20 minutes of showing some 50 outfits—coats, skirts, and dresses, matched with accessories such as hats, bags, and jewelry—the models lined up in two rows on the runway. Mizrahi came from behind the screen, walked between the rows, and waved to the applauding audience, smiling broadly. He ran back off the stage and into a swarm of cameras and journalists. With that, the show was over.

THE REVIEWS POUR IN

Mizrahi woke up the next morning and went to the newsstand nearest his apartment. He looked for the reviews to see if the show was considered a success. He read them and was thrilled. A *Women's Wear Daily* reviewer said, "Isaac Mizrahi really knows how to put on a show." *New York Times* fashion critic Bernadine Morris wrote:

> The show began with a brilliant theatrical move, as Mr. Mizrahi made the backstage action visible to his audience. Hairdressers, makeup people, and Mr. Mizrahi himself were seen fussing with the models. The designer had simply moved behind-the-scenes action to the stage . . . the runway seemed to explode when big plaid taffeta skirts appeared with gray sweatshirts in a totally different approach to the ball gown, and when clothes in colors like Nile green, orange, aqua, and lavender followed each other in a progression as showy as a Fourth of July display of fireworks. It was not a show you could forget.

He had made his comeback. Mizrahi had wrapped fur, high and low fashion, and brilliant colors together into a memorable performance of wearable art. He had taken pieces of his and other

Unlike other designers, Mizrahi does not focus soley on fashion. His interests, talents, and creative energy are also deeply rooted in the performing arts, and he has been in cabarets, on television and radio, and on the Internet.

cultures and made them into a statement that excited his audience. He hadn't created something out of nothing—he had uncovered, selected, and combined ideas to create something new. Like a poet, he had merged sights and sounds and sense, using fabric instead of words.

The reviewers in all the major fashion magazines understood what he had done and what look he was trying to achieve. After the show, he told reporters that it was all worthwhile and that he had a great sense of relief. He was now ready for his next challenge, the spring 1995 collection.

DESIGNING DREAMS

Fashion designer Ralph Lauren has famously said, "I don't design clothes, I design dreams." Mizrahi had designed dreams that were a reality. Like virtually all fashion designers, Mizrahi has an artistic temperament. Like all artists, he pays attention to color, detail, textures, patterns, and designs. He works in fabric and not oil paint, words, dance moves, or musical notes. His creativity flows until it overflows. But he told Marie Speed in an interview for *Success* magazine, "I never made the decision to be a fashion designer. It kind of picked me."

Like many artists, he is very sensitive to what is going on around him, constantly searching for raw material to transform into art. He takes something common and makes it into something uncommon.

And like many artists, he makes deep connections to others, especially in the New York City fashion design community. He needs others and learns from them. He is naturally sympathetic and compassionate. His circle of friends has a very large diameter.

Mizrahi embodies both art and entertainment: He is often called a born showman. Whether he was born or made for show business, he has succeeded not just as a designer. He loves and needs to talk, and he needs an audience of more than himself to listen. He is also a cabaret (a small nightclub) performer, a television/radio/Internet talk-show host and blogger, and even an author. In the process, he has become a celebrity. He often says he just likes to do a lot of things.

His career and his personal life often seem to be the same thing. His work is playful. In both work and play, he follows his instincts and listens carefully to his feelings. Those instincts and feelings let him see where he needs to go and what he needs to do to be successful. Speed wrote, "Mizrahi approaches his drive to do new things with a . . . belief that it is, indeed, all about the vision—and a versatility that started when he was very young." That vision and versatility began in the New York City borough known as Brooklyn, a place that is itself tireless and always moving forward.

2

Shaping a Designer

Mizrahi was born in Brooklyn on October 14, 1961. He is the youngest child and only son of Sarah and Zeke Mizrahi. The Mizrahis were part of a Syrian Jewish community numbering in the tens of thousands in New York City. Most went to temple and ate food influenced by Syrian cuisine, as did the Mizrahis.

Historian Johanna Neuman of the Jewish Virtual Library provided a bit of history for families like the Mizrahis: "Generations of czars and emperors in Europe over the centuries had stripped Jews of their connection to the land, restricting them to work as tailors or peddlers or bankers. Their very existence depended on their acumen [insight] at reading the needs and desires of the larger culture. That antenna for what would play . . . was the distinct advantage that smoothed their journey in fashion from worker bee to trendsetter." Neuman wrote that by the early 1900s, roughly 60 percent of all the Jews employed in New York City were working in the garment industry. And perhaps an even higher percentage in the Mizrahis' Brooklyn community had family ties to fashion.

Like computer people arriving in California's Silicon Valley in the 1980s, the garment industry workers in New York at the turn of the last century brought the right skills to a booming business at the right time. The recently invented Singer sewing machine made mass production of standard sizes of clothing possible. Before that, virtually all clothes were made by hand. In the late 1800s and early 1900s, this changed dramatically with Singer's invention.

Neuman also noted that fashion is a family business. Many designers, from Donna Karan to Kenneth Cole, had parents who worked in the industry. Isaac Mizrahi's father first worked as a pattern cutter on Wooster Street in New York City's Soho district. (Soho, an acronym for "South of Houston Street," is an area in southern Manhattan formerly known for its factories and still known for its lofts in cast-iron buildings.) Zeke Mizrahi eventually became a manufacturer of children's clothing.

Isaac Mizrahi's work-at-home mother also had a keen interest in fashion and culture. Mizrahi told *Women's Wear Daily* journalist Bridget Foley about his mother's early influence:

> She took me shopping everywhere, from Saks to Bergdorf Goodman to Loehmann's.... Her closet was filled with Norells, Balenciagas, Chanels. I'd go to her fittings when Saks had its custom shop. I have all these great memories of clothes: a Halston Ultra-Suede shirtdress; a Norman Norell ottoman jacket and crystal pleated chiffon pants. Those early years are so important; that's when you form your taste.

When he was only four, he noticed the daisy patterns on his mother's shoes. As the baby of the family and the only boy, he got his mother's special attention.

GROWING UP IN BROOKLYN

Brooklyn is the most heavily populated of New York City's five boroughs: If Brooklyn were a city unto itself, it would be the fourth largest in America. The borough is made up of many communities, some of which were part of the network of relationships that helped form young Isaac.

The family lived at first near Brooklyn's Ocean Parkway, a major road that stretches roughly 5 miles (8 kilometers) from Prospect Park to Coney Island. Home movies show Isaac as a very young child in a crib, bobbing up and down with such energy that the camera can't easily hold him in its sight. His energy fills the screen.

A few years later, the movies show him in a blue shirt and striped overalls on red-brick steps leading to his house. The house has small, green bushes in the front yard. He is not shy, looking directly at the camera. A white poodle watches from the yard.

When he was eight, the family moved to another section of Brooklyn called Midwood, in the south-central part of the borough. The houses there are usually larger than ones along Ocean Parkway—many have large front porches and two stories. And the feel is more suburban; tree-lined streets with lilacs, dogwoods, maples, and oaks were common. Blue jays and cardinals provided some of the loudest sounds at times.

Midwood was predominantly Jewish in the 1960s, but it was beginning a transition to the more diversified neighborhood it is today, with Chinese, Russian, Haitian, and Pakistani immigrants, along with people from many other cultures, moving in during the 1980s. Many famous people were born or have lived in Midwood, including Woody Allen, playwright Arthur Miller, Supreme Court Justice Ruth Bader Ginsburg, and actress Marisa Tomei. It also had more than a dozen yeshivas, or private Jewish schools. One of them, Yeshiva of Flatbush, became Isaac's elementary school in 1966.

A MISFIT AT SCHOOL

The Mizrahis wanted their son to have training in both Jewish (Judaic) studies and traditional liberal arts courses. The Yeshiva of Flatbush was very conservative. From a very early age, however, Isaac was anything but conservative. Young Isaac liked to do impersonations of the rabbis and make sketches of scenes from the Bible. Many of the sketches showed his interest in what clothes biblical characters were wearing. The teachers warned his parents that he was not normal. He was repeatedly suspended and expelled for being different. He was not a happy student. He was overweight and felt like an outsider. He says on his Web site, "I wanted to be drawing or painting or sewing. . . . I did not fit in at all."

But his parents would not give up on either their son or the school. Bridget Foley reported that his mother came to his rescue repeatedly. "His mother would unzip the high-style creation she had on that day, remove the red nail polish and jewelry, dig up some dowdy dress, and go to the Yeshiva, where she would . . . make a plea for sympathy."

Each time he was suspended or expelled, he was let back in after his mother made her case. He told Foley, "Once the school took me back, we'd go back home, she'd change her clothes and we'd go to lunch."

POP CULTURE KEEPS HIM COMPANY

Soon after he started school, Isaac come down with a life-threatening illness—spinal meningitis. The disease is an infection of the membranes surrounding the brain or spinal cord. Fortunately, a doctor named Bernard Greenberg at a medical center in Brooklyn diagnosed the bacterial infection and probably saved his life. Mizrahi remembers to this day sitting in the doctor's waiting room with all its puppets and toys. But the slow recovery from the illness only made him feel more separated from others. He began to retreat into a world of his own making that included puppets, television, and movies.

In a time before video games and personal computers, Isaac loved playing with puppets when he was very young. He sewed their clothes and gave shows for the neighbors. Like many sensitive children, he invented a play world. Just as Lewis Carroll's heroine Alice plunged down a rabbit hole into a world more interesting than her own, Isaac created an alternative, imaginary world in his parents' garage. What started as child's play ended up years later as a vocation.

His fantasies in that world were gradually replaced by popular culture, especially television. Mizrahi told interviewer Diane Clehane of Mediabistro.com that television "was always like my best friend. I loved reruns of *I Love Lucy*. . . . I grew up watching talk shows—I loved Merv Griffin, I loved Mike Douglas, I loved Johnny Carson." He liked the feeling of being part of a conversation. He told *New York Times* writer Lola Ogunnaike that his "biggest ambition in life was to be a great conversationalist." Early on, he knew he wanted to be a personality.

One of the women who inspired him was Mary Tyler Moore, the actress who played Mary Richards on *The Mary Tyler Moore Show*. Young Isaac and millions of others saw an unusual situation comedy: Mary Richards was not divorced, widowed, or looking for a man to support her. This was a unique concept for television in 1970. Something about it appealed greatly to young Isaac, and the movie *Unzipped* shows how he often makes references in his personal life to the character of Mary Richards. "You're going to make it after all," lyrics from the show's theme song, seemed like a wonderful motto.

ESCAPING INTO THE MOVIES

In 1968 Mizrahi went to see Barbra Streisand in the movie *Funny Girl*. He watched it with his family at the Ziegfeld Theater, and it made a great impression. After that, he began to do impressions of Streisand and other famous singers like Judy Garland and Dionne

Warwick. He told the story to *Index* magazine's Laurie Simmons: "And I used to have this following in the community where I grew up, in Brooklyn. . . . People used to stop me on the street [to do an impression of Streisand or other famous women]. . . . And it was always, 'Oh, you're fabulous,' but then, 'Ha-ha, what a freak.' That's what it was. . . . So when people say, 'Oh, you're this personality,' that's what I've always been and always will be."

Another movie that made a lasting impression was *Back Street* (the version released in 1961). A fashion designer, played by actress Susan Hayward, falls in love with a married man and must keep their relationship secret. In this movie, the fashion industry in New York is portrayed as glamorous and exciting, and Isaac noticed.

NEW TECHNOLOGY AND A NEW DIRECTION

Many accounts of Mizrahi's life say that his father bought him a sewing machine when he was 10 years old. Mizrahi's Web site says that in July 1972, his family was vacationing in New Jersey and he visited a Singer sewing machine store. He had saved money from babysitting and bought a secondhand sewing machine for $30. Whether this was a machine in addition to the one his father may have bought him, or the only one he now owned, the new technology helped change his direction in life.

He already liked to sew puppet clothing by hand, but now a new world was opened. Immediately he began to make clothes for his mother and her friends. They encouraged him at just the right time in his life, as did his father.

When he added machine attachments for making ruffles and other design features, he began to explore possibilities. And when he had his bar mitzvah in October 1974, his father gave him a pair of scissors with his name engraved on them.

Since he was very young, Isaac had played the piano and played it very well. But his piano teacher told him that he had to choose between studying the piano, being a performer, and making clothes. Isaac chose not to choose and continued all three. He never wanted to specialize, and he didn't like to be told what to do with his life.

But he did listen to a piece of advice from his favorite teacher at the yeshiva, Sheila Kanowitz. She knew him well. When he was getting close to graduating after eight difficult years, she said he belonged at the famous High School of Performing Arts in Manhattan (the school was informally known as PA). After auditioning and being accepted, he enrolled in September 1974, and his life changed immediately and forever.

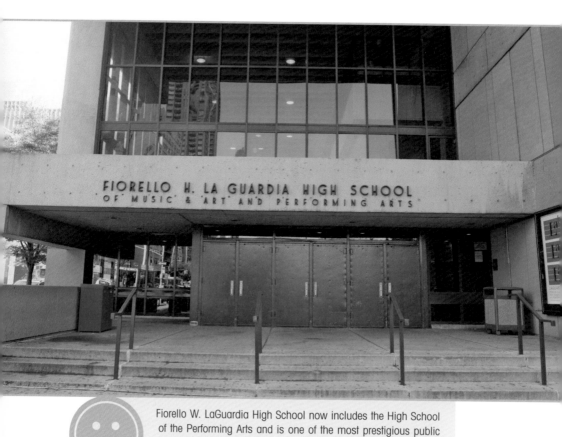

Fiorello W. LaGuardia High School now includes the High School of the Performing Arts and is one of the most prestigious public schools in New York City. Along with Mizrahi, the school's alumni include Jennifer Aniston, Adrien Brody, and Al Pacino.

A NEW SCHOOL BRINGS A NEW LIFE

PA was an alternative public high school on Manhattan's West Forty-sixth Street. It was for students gifted in the performing arts—primarily dance, drama, and instrumental music. Built in 1880, the old red-brick building with high ceilings and triangular windows became a kind of hall of fame. The combination of inspiration and perspiration required to succeed there has become the stuff of legend.

PA was the model for the fictional high school in the movie *Fame* (released in 1980, with a new version made in 2009) and a television series (from 1982 to 1987). Some graduates, like Al Pacino, Ving Rhames, Liza Minnelli, Omar Epps, Amy Ryan, and Marlon Wayans, would "light up the sky like a flame," as the movie's theme song describes. Others would not. The advertising line for *Fame* was "If they've really got what it takes, it's going to take everything they've got." It could have been the school's motto.

When Isaac arrived at PA in the fall of 1974, he was, as he described himself, "overweight, fat, [with] acne, horrible." He walked into a world of performers, where having an artistic temperament was not considered odd or abnormal. That was a culture shock, coming from the yeshiva. And this was his first exposure to Manhattan without his parents. That was a second shock to him.

The change did him a world of good. The first thing he did was get his weight under better control. He eventually lost 75 pounds (34 kg) and felt better about himself. He took speech classes and voice training, which also helped develop his confidence.

He had been accepted into PA in both music and drama. He told Foley, "I couldn't sit all day at the piano. It's too lonely. Acting was more related to fashion." It was because of this relationship that he chose to take more classes in the drama department.

Then, one day in July 1976, he experienced one of those moments that change a young life. He told Marie Speed in his interview for *Success*: "I was looking at the issue of *Vogue* that month—it was about the fall collection. It was the most fabulous thing; there was this portfolio of [fashion photographer Richard] Avedon photography, Patti

The Price of Fame

The High School of Performing Arts in New York got its start in the 1930s, when a high school principal heard music coming from his school's boiler room. He investigated and found four boys cutting class to rehearse their band. The principal, Dr. Franklin Keller, thought a different kind of high school for performers was needed. The school he started, with the help of New York mayor Fiorello La Guardia, became one of the most remarkable public high schools in American educational history.

Students first had to undergo a rigorous entrance exam and audition to get admitted. Then they were expected to take a full academic curriculum in addition to majoring in dance, drama, or instrumental music. For many, it was their first introduction to the passionate and unpredictable life in the arts. For some, it was their first introduction to hard work and high expectations.

The school inspired a film, *Fame*, that was released in 1980. In the movie, several students are followed from their first day to their last at the fictional New York Academy of Performing Arts. They blossom from children with dreams of being famous into young adults who take hold of their lives and use the arts to find, create, and express themselves. The characters have crises of confidence, problems with pushy parents, thoughts of suicide, sexual identity issues, and more.

Coco (played by Irene Cara) is a fiery singer and dancer whose talent and ambition are barely under control. Doris (Maureen Teefy) is shy at first and feels she has no personality, but she comes out of her shell, most famously at a midnight screening of the cult classic *Rocky Horror Picture Show*. And one of the characters, Touchstone, is played by Isaac Mizrahi.

A dance teacher in the movie says to her students, "You've got big dreams? You want fame? Well, fame costs. And right here is where you start paying—in sweat."

The Oscar-winning theme song has become part of our culture: "Fame! I'm gonna live forever!"

The real school did not live forever. In 1984, it was merged with another high school and moved to a new location. And in February 1988, the old red-brick building was destroyed by a fire.

Hansen and Janice Dickinson [two of the very first supermodels] in these unbelievable clothes. . . . I remember spending the whole night poring over that magazine and making the decision that I was going to do that." In the movie *Unzipped*, Mizrahi talks about "moments of revelation when you dare yourself to do something." He must have dared himself to make this career choice.

The school encouraged hands-on learning. In March 1978, at the age of 16, Isaac began sewing and designing on a larger scale. He formed a company that he named IS New York. His financial backer and mentor was family friend Sarah Haddad. The company was short-lived because Haddad's husband became very ill, but Isaac had made a very big first step into the real world of fashion.

The next step came when his father showed some of his sketches to designer Ellie Fishman. She suggested that Isaac was ready to start taking classes at night at the prestigious Parsons School of Design in Manhattan, so he did just that. He learned more and more, getting a jump on the next step in his education.

In June 1979, Isaac graduated from PA. He would later look back on his years there as some of the best of his life. He had come to PA as an immature outsider but was now accepted as an artist. That made all the difference.

By 1979, he had made the decision to pursue not acting but fashion design. He consulted a psychic at the time, the first of many, to help draw out his own feelings. He wrote in the *New York Times*: "The psychic's name was Guy Culver. I called him Madame Guy. The first thing he asked me was, 'Why did you leave show business?' . . . I was astounded that he knew I had studied acting and had recently made a conscious decision to go in another direction. By the end of the reading, I convinced myself that I was doing the right thing."

Around this time he also took the whirlwind trip of a young lifetime. He went to Paris to see one of the world's fashion capitals firsthand. He even designed a purple outfit and wore it on the flight. But he was apprehensive about being away from America for the first time, and he could barely sleep. In Paris, the pastry shops

After graduating from high school, Mizrahi began a formal education in fashion at the Parsons School of Design. Known as one of the top fashion schools in the country, Parsons nurtured Mizrahi's talents and connected him to his mentor, designer Perry Ellis.

opened early, and he was there when they opened. He soon saw and experienced everything he could about fashion and another culture as an American abroad. It was another chapter in his education.

THE PARSONS SCHOOL

In September 1979, Mizrahi enrolled at the Parsons School of Design full-time. One of its five divisions, the School of Fashion, has been called a training ground for Seventh Avenue. The school gave him access to some of the world's most advanced fashion design facilities. He took extensive courses on fashion design, the history of design, and the structure of textiles and fabric (including studying burn tests for each fabric).

Mizrahi was a brilliant student from the start. Teacher Maria Laveris says at her Web site, "Isaac would have been a gift to any teacher . . . he's the kind of student you would not forget, because he's a dream; both his character and his ability were outstanding." The chair of the fashion design department at the School of Fashion, Anne Keagy, eventually set up an appointment for Mizrahi with legendary designer Perry Ellis. He soon began working part-time as a design assistant under guidance from Ellis, who taught him more than he could say. In the interview with Speed, Mizrahi paid tribute to one of his most important mentors: "He was so incredibly fun to work with. He was such a shining example—he had amazing taste. I feel that everything I learned about textile came from Perry Ellis . . . the beauty, the luxury, the taste level of fabric, I got from Perry."

Mizrahi told Foley that Ellis "was a poet, a real artist. I loved him." Ellis couldn't sketch and wasn't the kind of hands-on designer that Mizrahi would become. But he was a shrewd businessman with innovative ideas about clean-cut and casual clothes and a great sense of marketing. He even taught Mizrahi a little about working with the fashion press.

In April 1982, Mizrahi was named one of eight Outstanding Student Designers at Parsons. The judges included famous

ELEMENTS OF STYLE

Mirrors, Lights, Actions

I can't stress enough the importance of having the right mirrors and lighting. Lighting is everything. Start being sensitive to it. When looking in a mirror, notice when the lighting is right and flatters you. Try to recreate that lighting as much as possible in your everyday world. It sounds ridiculous, but it's easier to plan ahead a little than to suffer the consequences of bad lighting. All actors and actresses understand this principal, and it's largely because of lighting that they look great all the time. You must have a full-length mirror; a three-way mirror would be heaven if you have the room. Your makeup mirror should be mounted in a well-lit location. Of course, a Hollywood style dressing-room mirror with small lightbulbs around all the sides would be fabulous. But I'm realistic, and a couple of well-placed desk lamps will do the trick. . . .

Look at pictures of yourself that you like and notice where the light source is coming from. Try to recreate that lighting all the time (not just when posing for pictures). . . . I always note the restaurants and hotels where the lighting is flattering . . . and go back often!

—*Isaac Mizrahi in* How to Have Style

designers Calvin Klein, Donna Karan, and Oscar de la Renta. His junior collection, a final project at the school, was videotaped to show future classes.

Around this same time, Mizrahi's father died. It must have been a painful blow, and his father would never get to see his son reach the height of his career. Zeke Mizrahi had always supported his son and had helped open the doors to his education.

When Mizrahi graduated from Parsons in the spring of 1983, his formal education was over. He was now ready to move further out into the world, to find his audience.

3

Creating a Famous Label

After Mizrahi graduated from Parsons, he was immediately hired by Perry Ellis International. He had proved himself to Ellis while working part-time: Ellis could often be heard asking that the student designer from Parsons be brought across the street to help with a certain show. Now Ellis had Mizrahi where he wanted him.

Mizrahi threw himself into the job. He told Foley, "I worked so hard. I used to think that I gave everything I had and he [Ellis] took. But in retrospect I know I took so much and he gave everything."

Tragedy struck when Ellis contracted AIDS. Many people in the early 1980s were so ignorant of the disease and how it spread that the company was afraid of letting the news out. The horrible disease wasn't well understood, and fear filled in the information

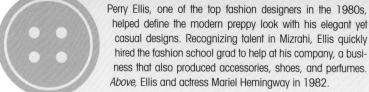

Perry Ellis, one of the top fashion designers in the 1980s, helped define the modern preppy look with his elegant yet casual designs. Recognizing talent in Mizrahi, Ellis quickly hired the fashion school grad to help at his company, a business that also produced accessories, shoes, and perfumes. *Above,* Ellis and actress Mariel Hemingway in 1982.

gaps. The company worried that people might not want to buy Ellis's clothes for fear of becoming infected. Soon, the haunting shadow of death from AIDS loomed over the entire fashion industry. Ellis died in 1986. Mizrahi still thinks of him as a guardian angel watching over him.

Jeffrey Banks Ltd., well known for its menswear, hired Mizrahi in 1985 to help design a new women's wear collection. But Banks's parent company withdrew some financial backing, and Mizrahi quickly moved on to Calvin Klein. He helped create one of the company's more interesting collections, highlighted by stream-lined red suits. Mizrahi told Foley that Klein "has a great eye. He's hardworking and knows just what he wants. He's very dominant." But Mizrahi again moved on quickly. Klein, he said, "knew I was just passing through."

STARTING A NEW LABEL

Mizrahi's obvious talent and drive were too much for any one company to hold on to him. And Mizrahi was never one to fit into a corporate culture easily. He stood out and had strong opinions. In June 1987, Mizrahi, with the help of his former backer, Sarah Haddad (now Sarah Haddad-Cheney), started his own company. They each invested $50,000 and located the business in a loft on Greene Street in Soho.

Mizrahi painted the walls and built the tables, doing everything a small business owner who is hands-on needs to do. He then made and showed some clothes there to potential buyers in September 1987 in a small fashion show, his very first. His goal was to take some features of evening wear and extend them to day wear, combining the two very different looks. And in a move that he was to become famous for, he combined the expensive and the inexpensive. He loved women who wore $2,000 cashmere coats with a $20 T-shirt.

He sold roughly 50 pieces to several stores, including famous New York department stores Saks Fifth Avenue and Bloomingdale's. He also showed and delivered his handmade garments from the backseat of Haddad-Cheney's car. He gave "trunk shows," displaying his collection to select groups, first at the department store Bergdorf Goodman. Business was picking up, and fashion insiders began to notice.

He soon expanded his business to other well-known department stores, including Neiman Marcus, with garments made for the spring of 1988. But his first real breakthrough collection was the one he made and showed in April 1988 for the fall.

THE BREAKTHROUGH SHOW

His inspiration for the look and the show had come from the Shakespeare play *King Lear*. On his Web site's timeline, he says, "I love the sense of the cold, of wanting people wrapped in layers of woolens." It was a theme he would vary for his famous comeback show in April 1994: The ancient protective role of clothing and its ability to both hide and reveal always interested him. He always wanted to tap into deeper human needs, not just superficial wants. And he wanted to combine looks. In this case, he combined the youthful and the sophisticated. He also played with bright colors and traditional fabrics.

Two flights up from his studio in Soho, a few members of the press gathered with his growing client base of retailers in-the-know. The show began, and by its end, the fashion world really began to pay attention to this new creative force. His 50 garments for both day and evening wear were magic. Bridget Foley reported for *Women's Wear Daily* that the April 1988 show was a hit for the insiders lucky enough to know about it:

> The talk of SA [Seventh Avenue] is Isaac Mizrahi, a 26-year-old alumnus of Parsons School of Design, former apprentice to Perry Ellis and Calvin Klein, a bit player in the movie *Fame* and once the Peck's Bad Boy of Yeshiva Flatbush in Brooklyn.
>
> Mizrahi showed a fall collection that struck a smart balance between youthful exuberance and sophistication. It wowed the crowd. Retailers left raving.
>
> Joan Kaner, vice president of Macy's New York, called it "one of the best shows here or in Europe."

Mizrahi's Web site timeline states that during this show, "I was in another world. I was so intensely focused on the girls [his models]. I was so focused on making them look beautiful. I never noticed the show go by. I recollect nothing except the show ending and the applause."

The fashion world, like any entertainment industry, is always in search of the new. Mizrahi in 1988 was the new, going from unknown to known on Seventh Avenue in only a matter of months. He was called a rising star for mixing unusual bright colors and patterns into simple glamour. He paid attention to details and put on a good show.

But Mizrahi dismissed talk that he was a star. He said that would take years of performance. He told Foley his goal "is not to achieve tremendous commercial success, but to develop a language and a style with clothes." When all those around him were losing their heads about how famous he was going to be, he kept his accomplishments in perspective. Mostly he worked very hard, usually 18 hours a day. He was only half joking when he said that if he had to polish the runway at his next show with his own hands, he would do it.

THE BUSINESS GROWS

Mizrahi's second major collection was shown in October 1988. This time, everyone in the fashion world knew about it. Woody Hochswender of the *New York Times* wrote that "the scene resembled a nightclub opening. The fashion throng milled around a single doorway on lower Broadway near Houston, fighting to get in. Inside, the press and retail executives . . . shrieked and swooned with delight."

The attention was a public relations dream come true. All of a sudden, Mizrahi's clothes were featured in *Elle, Harper's Bazaar,* and *Vogue.* Everyone agreed that the reasons for his success included his colorful design sense, his outgoing and over-the-top personality that made writing about him fun and fashionable, and his incredible attention to the details of putting together a show. He cast the best models and made sure their makeup and hair were perfect for the look he wanted. His styles looked great on the runway. His theatrical sense was perfect—he had a flair for the dramatic.

The very small business grew like a hothouse flower. His company went from producing a few hundred garments in 1987 to

3,500 for 1988 and 12,000 in 1989. Mizrahi's sales almost tripled every year, from $500,000 in revenue in 1987 to $1.5 million in 1988 and $4 million in 1989.

Mizrahi was proud that all of his clothes were made in the United States. He told Hochswender, "The better factories can see we're growing, and it's easier to get them to work with us. I'm thrilled with the way the clothes are coming out of the factories."

He also now had a new financial backer, Haim Dabah, who was building Gitano jeans into a fashionable but budget-conscious label. He was even getting offers to license his name (designers sell their names and sometimes their expertise to producers of handbags, perfumes, and other fashion items for a percentage of the profits). His career spiraled upward.

THE FIRST MAJOR AWARDS

Acclaim was something he was going to have to get used to. In November 1988, the Council of Fashion Designers of America (CFDA, the major organization representing the fashion industry) awarded Mizrahi the Perry Ellis Award for Emerging Talent. Each year, the CFDA gives out awards for Designer of the Year in women's wear and menswear, an Emerging Talent Award, a Lifetime Achievement Award, and more. These are often called the "Oscars of fashion." The awards are voted on by fashion writers and retailers.

Interestingly, no award was given that year for the Designer of the Year for women's wear, the most coveted award. Rumor had it that both Ralph Lauren and Donna Karan had been close, but disagreements among the 15 fashion journalists and retailers who voted couldn't be resolved. The CFDA, like any organization, had politics.

The prestigious Emerging Talent Award was handed to Mizrahi on January 9, 1989, at a gala dinner at New York's Metropolitan Museum of Art. The party after the dinner lasted well into the night.

Many people felt that the emerging talent award could be a kiss of death. Often designers who won it never won anything else. But Mizrahi was not a one-year wonder. His 1989 collections were as well

ELEMENTS OF STYLE

Learning how to have style is all about learning to express yourself. It requires an I-deserve-it attitude and plenty of self-confidence. . . .

To create your own style, think about yourself and take pleasure when shopping. When most people go shopping, the immediate response is to get it over with. "Okay, I'll take it" is too often the reaction, without giving any thought as to why you're buying that particular item. Instead, stop and ask yourself, "Where does this dress/handbag/sweater fit in my life?" If you don't have a good reason for buying it, put it back. . . .

Don't be afraid of colors. Experiment with them. Just as you have to try on a lot of clothes to find the shape that is perfect for you, you have to try on clothes in lots of different colors too. Play with colors that you think might clash. Remember how your mother told you never to wear orange and pink together? She was so wrong. That's one of my favorite color combinations. Consider wearing all one color or several shades of a particular hue from top to bottom. Use accessories for extra color.

—*Isaac Mizrahi in* How to Have Style

received as any he had done. The next year he capped off his sudden rise to acclaim by winning the Designer of the Year for women's wear. The award was presented by CFDA president Carolyne Roehm on February 6, 1990, at the Metropolitan Museum. So many people wanted to be on the guest list that the planned dance floor had to be eliminated to put in more tables. When Mizrahi won the same award again in 1991, he became one of the elite group of multiple winners, including Donna Karan (1990, 1996), Calvin Klein (1987, 1993), Narciso Rodriguez (2002, 2003), Oscar de la Renta (2000, 2007), Francisco Costa (2006, 2008), and Marc Jacobs (1992, 1997).

The acclaim of winning the awards raises the profile of a designer and helps business, much as winning an Oscar helps a movie at the box office. More stores now knew and bought the Mizrahi label, which meant that more customers did as well. Nothing goes out of a store without first coming in. His line had precious space on the sales floors of the biggest department stores and some specialty stores as well. But every silver lining has a cloud, and some storm clouds began to gather over Mizrahi's fashion parade.

GROWING PAINS

In February 1989, fashion writer Woody Hochswender raised the issue of how successful Mizrahi's business actually was. He asked the question: "Is Mizrahi a superstar or a shooting star? Will the clothes that caused such emotion on the runway translate into sales on the retail floor?" Some retail executives told Hochswender that some of Mizrahi's fabrics looked good on the runway but not on hangers in stores. Mizrahi acknowledged to Hochswender that his business was having growing pains. "Quality problems are part of being a designer. People expect quality. But hanger appeal? Sometimes the most interesting clothes only look interesting when you put them on."

He started to shop around for new factories after receiving shipments of poorly made clothes. Some he could not ship to stores. But he became even more determined to get better at his business.

Bridget Foley followed up with an interview at Mizrahi's apartment a few months later, in May 1989. She also raised the issue of the Mizrahi business:

> Despite all of the Isaac-as-fashion-deity hoopla during the past year, Mizrahi also has been the recipient of a few hard knocks. . . . Painful were allegations questioning the quality and sell-through [the number of garments a store actually sells to customers at full price as opposed to how many they buy from the designer] of last fall's collection.
>
> "A couple of times my mother went into Bloomingdale's or Bergdorf's and said she saw something that didn't look the money," says Mizrahi. "Now, I'm really conscious of it."

The criticism that most hurt Mizrahi was that he had borrowed some design ideas from others. He told Foley, "Maybe some designers open up issues of *Vogue* from the Sixties and copy; I don't. But maybe I did something that ended up looking like something someone else had done. Big deal. . . . Life is about a recurrence of style."

He was now a target, for better or worse. Fashion is a big business, and some of his competitors were now protecting their turf.

THE DESIGNER AT HOME

Bridget Foley's May 1989 interview had lighter moments. She reported that Mizrahi had moved in 1988 to Chelsea from Manhattan's Upper West Side and was feeling the difference between the two parts of his beloved city. The Upper West Side had more of a neighborhood atmosphere, but he loved his "graceful old Chelsea apartment, water-damaged ceilings and all."

Foley noted that he had a tartan (plaid) wing chair next to a fireplace, a white card table and chairs, and a pair of thrift shop lamps without shades in his living room. He was not living in grand style. He had ordered a pumpkin-colored couch and some green and navy curtains, so help was on the way.

Mizrahi said he made conscious choices not to put on airs: "Who needs another pretty face with an opinion?" But he does love to entertain. And even small parties at his place are a big deal. He can't have a casual get-together: "Every single linen. Every single piece of china has to come out. It's like a bar mitzvah."

When Foley commented on his plaid jacket and tartan wing chair, he said, "I've always loved tartans. Perry (Ellis) loved them. That influenced me." Foley wrote that Mizrahi doesn't like to wax on about inspiration. "A, it's too personal. B, it sounds too artsy-craftsy. That's not what clothes are supposed to be about—tortured artists."

But he talked about the pride that comes with wearing some clothes. Ancient societies with their togas, kilts, and saris fascinate him. And the tension between "barbaric" and "civilized" societies and their clothing styles always makes him think and wonder.

GETTING A MANAGEMENT TEAM

Just as Apple computers had to hire professional managers after it got to a certain size, Isaac Mizrahi & Co. did as well. Professional managers introduce systems for quality and inventory control, forecasting, and financial help. And they focus not just on sales but on profits. Some in the industry claimed that by 1991, Mizrahi was successful in many ways but not making a profit.

When Jennifer Peck was hired as a vice president of Isaac Mizrahi in 1991, she had been a successful executive at Ralph Lauren. Now, she could bring the designer her management skills. She immediately helped improve quality control and lowered costs and prices. She built in better computer tracking systems. She also became a sounding board for ideas. And she stressed that Mizrahi had to achieve more of a consistent look, a predictable shape and color scheme that designers like Ralph Lauren, Donna Karan, and Calvin Klein were marketing well. He needed to become a brand.

Peck noticed something as soon as she came on board. She summarized to Cathy Horyn in the *Washington Post* the difference between her current boss and her former boss: "Isaac is a true designer. Ralph [Lauren] has a design team of 75 people, and I don't think any of them has a technical background. I have the greatest respect for Ralph and what he's done, but it's a different thing. It's more about styling and marketing. The key thing with Isaac is that he actually sketches. All these things come from his head."

Women's Wear Daily reported in August 1992 that Mizrahi's professional approach was beginning to show. Kal Ruttenstein at Bloomingdale's told *Women's Wear Daily*, "He's really selling well this season. I attribute this to his maturing as a designer . . . [and] deliveries have been very good and the quality has improved greatly." Both Saks and Bloomingdale's reported that Mizrahi's wool and tweed jackets and skirts were flying out of the stores.

Soon after Peck arrived, so did a new major investor. In 1992, Chanel Inc. bought a substantial stake in Mizrahi's company. That came as a big help since one of Mizrahi's biggest backers, Haim

Dabah, had recently declared bankruptcy; his Gitano jeans company had expanded too fast in a slowing economy. Chanel could also provide advice about building a brand. Mizrahi told Cathy Horyn that with this help, he could learn "not to be obsessed with the things I shouldn't be obsessed with. When I started this company ... I was such a mess—about financial matters ... about everything. And that makes it hard to concentrate on what neckline you want."

AN AMERICAN DESIGNER

His business sense got more sophisticated as a result of learning from the new management team. Mizrahi now began talking more in public about his company's identity and about being an American designer. Foley reported that Mizrahi had declared independence from Europe. "I'm so tired with American designers copying the Europeans. It sickens me. I think we've lost that classic New York look. ... But we're starting to regain that attitude of ease."

Mizrahi tried to explain what an American design look was. "Europeans—they live in an ancient culture. They can rightfully decorate things. They come from a long line of decorators. They went to school for that. I didn't. I went to school to learn how to create purity." For him, purity was simplicity and a focus on clothes and not accessories like watches, handbags, and hats. He was trying for a "bold, no-nonsense, clean" look in which color and shape interact. "I'm really stressing shape. Feminine shapes in beautiful colors. It's not ... a bunch of accessories and a bunch of hair and a bunch of makeup."

He had always been known for his lively, upbeat colors. He told Foley, "beautiful color is such an important part of life. I love black and white, but we don't see in black and white. We see in color."

By the end of 1994, journalist Cathy Horyn was writing that Mizrahi's designs were "purely, almost ecstatically, American: the parka, the jumper, the desert boot, the boatneck dance dress. But more than his breezy shapes and offhand sense of styling, Mizrahi had color—clear, bracing combinations of violet, periwinkle, and jade." Mizrahi stressed to Horyn his desire to have an American appeal. "I still want to do eye-popping clothes, but I don't want them to be sight gags. Right now, that's what European fashion is about. Sight gags. I'm sorry. Period."

FASHION'S TWO CATEGORIES

Mizrahi's American designs tended to be a combination of more casual sportswear with touches of high style and glamour. The fashion world distinguishes between two kinds of clothes: haute couture (or just *couture*) and ready-to-wear. Haute couture is very high-end, custom clothing made by hand of the highest quality material for special clients. For a design company to be considered an haute couture house, it must belong to the Syndical Chamber for Haute Couture, a Paris-based group governed by the French Department of Industry. The house must show collections twice yearly, each with at least 35 separate outfits.

Ready-to-wear clothes are almost everything that is not couture. They can be bought in stores and so are not custom made. Ready-to-wear is usually broken down into two categories: designer collections made of higher-quality fabrics and better construction methods for a higher price, and mass-market collections, usually with lower-quality fabrics and construction and a lower price. The designer collections are most often sold in department and specialty stores, and mass-market collections are sold in discount stores and factory outlets.

The fashion world sometimes makes similar distinctions for items other than garments (also called wearing apparel). Footwear and accessories (handbags, jewelry, scarves, and more) are often referred to as designer level and mass-market level, but not usually as couture or ready-to-wear.

THE FASHION INDUSTRY GETS A BLACK EYE

The fashion industry has a lot in common with the film industry. Both are dream factories that sell powerful images. Both are big businesses, making billions of dollars each year (but the fashion industry has greater revenues than the film industry, bringing in

Funny Face, starring Audrey Hepburn and Fred Astaire (*above*), is a classic musical film about fashion and romance. Astaire's character, Dick Avery, is loosely based on famous fashion photographer Richard Avedon, who consulted on the film.

at least 20 times as much money). Both have creative and talented leaders who try to motivate a large number of people to carry out a vision. And both are filled with people who don't want or aren't able to work anywhere else.

In 1994 and 1995, two films about the fashion industry appeared: Robert Altman's *Prêt-à-Porter* (released in the United States as *Ready-to-Wear*) and Douglas Keeve's *Unzipped*. Altman's film pokes fun at the entire fashion industry. It takes place in one of the world's fashion capitals, Paris, during Fashion Week. Altman shows frantic designers, temperamental and vain models (including Naomi Campbell, Linda Evangelista, Carla Bruni, and Christy Turlington), high-powered and ruthless magazine editors who are bitter rivals, clueless writers, photographers who like to humiliate models, hard-shopping rich people, and much more.

The film gives no mercy to the fashion world. At the end of the movie, models come down the runway with no clothes. The shock value hid the fact that the film had little in the way of plot or subtlety. The movie quickly faded out of sight and is considered one of Altman's worst films.

THE FASHION INDUSTRY'S VALENTINE

Ready-to-Wear gave way to *Unzipped* in movie theaters a few months later. Director Douglas Keeve had been a fashion photographer and Mizrahi's boyfriend for several years when he began filming the designer for a documentary. He had never made a movie, but he had unprecedented access to his subject. Amy Spindler of the *New York Times* interviewed Mizrahi before the movie came out. She wrote:

> "*Unzipped* is going to tell the fashion industry that you don't necessarily have to be a snob to have really good taste or design clothes," Mr. Mizrahi said. "For years, people have equated designers with people who don't think and people who have a lot of attitude and people who throw fits. It's going to prove fashion designers are human beings...."
>
> The moral of his personal tale, he said, is that fashion is more like cooking than an art form. "It's about assembling great and fresh ingredients and recognizing that it's about appetite."

Keeve pitched his movie idea to many people, looking for financing. Spindler later wrote that his pitch was simple: Mizrahi was "the media darling of the fashion industry. He's the funniest person on earth. He's so interesting and compelling.... Everybody's excited about fashion. We've got models. We've got a show. We've got pizzazz." Keeve told interviewers and possible backers that fashion people "are some of the most intelligent, complex, worldly people that exist today in our culture. Their antenna is always up. They're always seeing things, pulling things in from the outside world." With Mizrahi as the draw, Keeve finally got a green light for production and filmed Mizrahi for more than six months.

Unzipped was released on August 11, 1995. It was a hit with audiences and critics alike. Janet Maslin of the *New York Times* called it a "valentine to the fashion world in general and this irrepressible [unsinkable] designer in particular." Most moviegoers and reviewers were touched by scenes in which Sarah Mizrahi says while admiring some garments, "My Isaac made this." She states it with such pride that even Mizrahi seems a little embarrassed.

Maslin wrote that "*Unzipped* builds its tension until it reaches the big day [of the April 1994 show]. It looks on as Mr. Mizrahi changes from life of the party into drill sergeant, frantically finishing the clothes." Recalling that in *Ready-to-Wear* the models come down the runway at the end of the movie naked, Maslin wrote, "*Unzipped* doesn't have to be that unzipped. It knows why clothes work better."

A NEW LINE FOR EVERYDAY STARS

After *Unzipped*, Mizrahi was such a hot designer that some of the most famous actresses were wearing his creations to various awards shows. Actress Nicole Kidman wore a beautiful pale blue beaded gown for the Fifty-third Golden Globe Awards in January 1996. Julia Roberts showed up in a black Mizrahi dress to accept a People's Choice award in January 1998, and Helen Hunt wore a Mizrahi creation in pale pink for the Golden Globes the same month.

Mizrahi took advantage of his fame and new celebrity status. He helped launch not only *Unzipped* but a brand-new line of clothing at the same time. In August 1995, he toured the country advertising both his movie and his new collection, named IS**C. The clothes were part of a bridge line (also called a secondary line); a bridge line markets a designer's vision with clothes that are more affordable. It bridges the two kinds of ready-to-wear garments, the designer collection and the mass-market collection.

Mizrahi trademarked the phrase "American Star Quality" as the tagline for his advertising of the new branch of the company. He chose two stars to replace the two As in his name because he wanted to reinforce the idea that fashion is entertainment and that "every woman is a star." He may have also played on the similarity of asterisks and daisies, a special symbol that recalled his first memories of the daisies on his mother's shoes.

Mizrahi told Bridget Foley of *Women's Wear Daily* in an August 3, 1995, interview, "I'm talking about forms of American

Hollywood and the Fashion Industry

Hollywood has long been fascinated by the fashion industry. From the 1939 movie *The Women*, with a six-minute fashion parade, to the comedies *Bruno* and *Zoolander*, to *Lipstick*, *Coco Before Chanel*, and *Valentino: The Last Emperor*, dozens of movies have featured the business of fashion.

But three movies stand out. *Unzipped* is one. Another is the musical *Funny Face* (1957). Maggie Prescott (played by Kay Thompson) is a demanding, high-powered fashion magazine editor. She and her most famous photographer, Dick Avery (Fred Astaire), are looking for a fresh face for the magazine, someone both intellectual and beautiful. They somehow find the shy wallflower Jo Stockton (Audrey Hepburn) selling books in a small Greenwich Village bookshop. Jo has contempt for the superficial world of fashion. But, as movie fate would have it, she is soon flown to Paris by Prescott and Avery and becomes a supermodel. She is transformed, just like Cinderella, and even finds true love (with Avery).

A five-minute montage of Hepburn in Paris on a fashion shoot is a cinema classic. The sequence was designed by fashion photographer Richard Avedon, the model for Dick Avery and one of Mizrahi's idols. Two of the most lasting images from the movie are Hepburn

Star Quality—circuses, arcades, video games, movie stars. I want this to be about fun and enthusiasm in dressing." Mizrahi listed the "basic needs" of any young woman: a diverse lineup of denim, the right sweats, short shorts, a checked suit, and a little black dress.

Mizrahi chose hot pink as a color theme. "Pink is more than a color. It's an emotion. It represents something significant—fresh, positive, and incredible."

He and Jennifer Peck, now the president of his company, had high hopes for the new line. So did Chanel, still his main financial

coming down a long staircase in a flowing red gown and her wearing a beatnik look—tight black slacks and a black turtleneck—during a dance number at a Parisian coffeehouse.

Prescott is loosely based on two legendary figures in fashion, *Vogue*'s Diana Vreeland and *Harper's Bazaar*'s Carmel Snow. One of the songs from the musical, "Think Pink," seems to have been a source of inspiration for Mizrahi.

The third movie is *The Devil Wears Prada* (2006). Andy Sachs (played by Anne Hathaway) is a recent college graduate who wants to be a journalist. She lands a job as a junior assistant to the icy, brilliant, eccentric, demanding editor of *Runway* magazine, Miranda Priestly (played by Meryl Streep). Priestly's silver hair and pale skin make her resemble a kind of white witch, a villainess who sends Andy on nearly impossible missions like finding copies of an unpublished Harry Potter novel.

The fashion industry is portrayed as cutthroat and filled with backstabbing and sucking up. But Andy gets good at her job, becomes much more stylish, and finally even escapes into a better job. And Priestly ends up being an almost sympathetic character, obviously filled with love for her two daughters and willing to sacrifice herself to be a driving force in the industry.

The inspiration for Miranda Priestly was reportedly current *Vogue* editor Anna Wintour. Most designers and models were afraid to appear in the movie for fear of damage to their careers. Only designer Valentino and model/*Project Runway* host Heidi Klum appear as themselves. Wintour actually ended up liking the movie, so designers and models needn't have been afraid.

investor, owning some 70 percent of Isaac Mizrahi & Co. Mizrahi was now doing business with big budgets and big expenses.

LOVING NEW YORK

Writer Ruth La Ferla spent some time with Mizrahi and wrote in late 1997 about a museum visit they made to the International Center of Photography. One photograph caught Mizrahi's attention: It was called "Sam Karshowitz, Rag Peddler." The old photo showed a weary salesman who had come in from an ice storm. Mizrahi stopped and stared, then said, "Now he had a life."

He looked at various old photos of rich people with top hats and fur coats, of homeless people wearing rags, and lovers holding hands. He came to a photograph titled "A Waterfront Shooting," showing a murder scene. The bloody victim lay on the sidewalk while his grieving family clutched each other. Mizrahi said the picture "says more about life than death. It doesn't make me want to cry. I want to be involved."

He looked at pictures of firemen, showgirls, and drag queens. He said, "The city is a jungle in all its savagery and refinement. And that's what you love about it—just being part of it, swinging from vine to vine."

Mizrahi told La Ferla about his life in New York. He loved going to Chanterelle, a fancy restaurant (now closed), in a neighborhood known as Tribeca (an acronym for "Triangle Below Canal Street"), south of Soho. But he loved having a hot dog on the street as well. On Monday evenings he said he liked to go to the exclusive Manhattan Bridge Club on West Seventy-second Street. Mizrahi told of a man who recently walked "into the room with his briefcase, and he just stands in the doorway, and you can see in his eyes that he's a little bit afraid. When I look at him, I almost burst into tears."

Mizrahi became philosophical. "You end up wanting what you've chosen, and that's a discovery." Whether he chose fashion design or it had chosen him, he wanted what he had. And he had chosen to live in New York City, a jungle of eagerness, hustle, and

Directed by Mizrahi's then-boyfriend, documentary film-maker Douglas Keeve, *Unzipped* is a behind-the-scenes look at the fashion world. The film focuses on Mizrahi's efforts to create the looks and organize a fashion show for his comeback Fall 1994 collection. Supermodels Naomi Campbell (*left*) and Linda Evangelista (*right*) were both in Mizrahi's fashion show and were featured in the film.

flow that nourished him. If it also contained broken people with broken dreams, he wasn't one of them.

Writer E.B. White wrote about New York, "It is to the nation what the white church spire is to the village—the visible symbol of aspiration [ambition] and faith." But White also wrote about the anxiety that the city could produce. High aspirations mixed with high anxieties defined Mizrahi well.

HIGH VISIBILITY

High visibility, to go along with aspirations and anxieties, also helped define Mizrahi in the 1990s. He designed costumes for plays and theater. He was even nominated for an Emmy Award for his costumes for Liza Minnelli's *Live from Radio City* television concert in December 1992.

He had won CFDA awards, including a special one for *Unzipped*, and many other prizes. He won Designer of the Year by the Italian Trade Commission in 1994 and Cadillac's Award of Excellence for American Design the same year. He was called "Le Miz" by *Women's Wear Daily*. Fashion journalist Cathy Horyn wrote, "No other designer of his generation was more destined to succeed than Isaac Mizrahi."

He was getting rich and famous on an international scale. In 1997, he signed agreements for stores and distributors in Japan, Singapore, and Korea. And Mizrahi's designs were on fashion magazine covers constantly in the 1990s, including a *Harper's Bazaar* cover featuring Linda Evangelista in March 1997 and the cover of *Cosmopolitan* two months later. Supermodel Claudia Schiffer wore a white Mizrahi dress on the June 1998 cover of the same magazine. Demi Moore wore Mizrahi designs on the pages of *Vanity Fair*.

AUTHOR AND ACTOR

Mizrahi is also highly versatile. By the late 1990s, he was both an author and a movie actor.

In 1997, he published three comic books bound in one volume with the title *Isaac Mizrahi Presents the Adventures of Sandee the Supermodel*. The graphic narrative is about a tall and beautiful blonde from Bountiful, Utah, who is discovered by the thin and handsome designer Yvesaac Mizrahi in a New York coffee shop. She becomes a cover model and then a supermodel with the help of her discoverer and mentor. But on the road to success, Sandee struggles with an eating disorder and with being treated badly by several people in the fashion industry, including agents, photographers, publicists, and magazine editors. She triumphs in the end, starring in a movie that wins an Academy Award.

Mizrahi began working on a film based on Sandee's exploits, to be funded by DreamWorks Studio. Actor Mike Myers was reportedly ready to sign as the male lead. *Women's Wear Daily* reported that Mizrahi was working with director Barry Sonnenfeld and Disney on another project as well. These projects seem to have been left in development.

And Mizrahi fulfilled a dream by becoming an actor in a Woody Allen film. In 1997, he played a stubble-faced artist named Bruce Bishop in a film named *Celebrity* (released in 1998). He would soon play a chef in Allen's *Small Time Crooks*. His ties to the film industry that began with *Unzipped* were getting stronger and more binding.

FIRE AND ICE

Big Hollywood parties are legendary. Mizrahi was part of one on December 3, 1997, when he presented his spring 1998 collection at the Fire and Ice Ball, one of the great social events of the year.

The party took place in a tent almost the length and width of a football field on the Paramount Studios lot. An artificial lagoon was constructed in the middle of it, making it look like an old movie musical set. Mizrahi's models could glide down the runway that stretched over the lagoon, giving the illusion they were walking on water.

Hollywood studio executives and actors from Sherry Lansing to Tom Hanks and Rita Wilson, Halle Berry, and Salma Hayek mingled with fashion industry power players, including Revlon chair Ronald Perlman and Saks Fifth Avenue chair Phillip Meyer. Mizrahi was one of the event's cochairs. The party, like many of Hollywood's biggest, was a fund-raiser: $2 million was collected for the Revlon/UCLA Women's Cancer Research program.

Mizrahi has said that sometimes women want to look completely different at night and play a role. So parties like the Fire and Ice Ball usually pose more fashion challenges for women than for men. "Black tie" on the invitation means the men wear tuxedos, but women have a much wider range of options, from black suits to lavish gowns designed by Versace or Mizrahi. And the gowns alone can evoke images of fairy tale princesses, Hollywood actresses, or femme fatales, depending on the role chosen.

Another challenge for the female Hollywood partygoer is that actresses know how to "glam up" with hair and makeup experts at their side. That can be intimidating for female executives and wives with no such team behind them. They want to dress up but not look overly done up.

But in the world of grand parties, fashion, and fame, nothing is forever—especially in Hollywood. With the Fire and Ice Ball, Mizrahi was standing at the intersection of Hollywood and Seventh Avenue. That can be a dangerous place. Only a few months after the Fire and Ice Ball, his career would crash.

4

Wounded and Recovering

Jennifer Peck had warned Mizrahi. He needed to be more consistent and develop a brand, a signature look that didn't vary much from year to year. She had looked at the numbers and seen that his sell-through, the percentage of clothes bought by a store that actually sell to customers at full price, was lower than it needed to be. He was selling 50 to 60 percent of his clothes at the retail price, not the 70 to 80 percent of Donna Karan, Giorgio Armani, or Ralph Lauren. Those designers had looks that didn't vary much from year to year. Kal Ruttenstein, the fashion director at Bloomingdale's, told Mizrahi, "It's nice to have powder blue parkas in your line, but make sure you also have the blazers and skirts that people will buy."

The IS**C line had not taken off. It was expensive to launch, requiring large advertising and sales costs, and had not lived up to expectations. The bridge line dragged down his company's profits. He had to close IS**C in late 1997. It was a sign of things to come.

In late 1998, the long upward spiral of success suddenly turned downward. The loss of IS**C meant that Isaac Mizrahi & Co. was not going to have an expected sales volume and profit. Soon, his main backer, Chanel, began talks with him about what needed to happen for them to stay in business with him. Profits needed to pick up. For many reasons—an Asian economic collapse, the low sell-through, and the lack of profitable licenses for items like perfumes—they didn't.

A MORTAL WOUND FOR ISAAC MIZRAHI & CO.

In late September 1998, Chanel told Mizrahi that it was withdrawing its investment in Isaac Mizrahi & Co. It wasn't personal, it was business. He was devastated. He now had three choices, as he explained to *People* magazine: "One was operating on a shoestring. Another was finding other backers. The third was closing. I thought, 'Move on darling, move on.'"

On October 1, 1998, Mizrahi had one of the worst days of his life. He had to tell his 55 employees that Chanel was withdrawing support and he had to close his beloved business. Some of the people had been with him for all 11 years of the company's existence. Most were shocked. Some couldn't stop crying.

The next day, the *New York Times* had a front-page article by Constance White announcing the closing. It was headlined, "Mizrahi, Designer Most Likely to Succeed, Doesn't." White wrote, "Despite the creativity and irrepressible personality for which Mr. Mizrahi was known to fashion insiders, he failed to create a signature image ... with which average shoppers could identify." Liz Tilberis, the editor in chief of *Harper's Bazaar*, told White, "It's very sad. A smile has gone out of the fashion industry. But the saddest part is that we are headed toward a kind of mediocrity."

The shock waves spread throughout the industry, especially to the stores that depend on designers like Mizrahi. Kal Ruttenstein

ELEMENTS OF STYLE

When it comes to buying clothes, think like an art collector who buys paintings from a particular period or artist. Collectors become intimately knowledgeable about their areas of expertise. They visit galleries and auction houses to study paintings. If a specific work is appealing, they ask for a photograph or transparency so they can study it. Sometimes they buy a painting; other times they miss out on a purchase because it's been sold to another collector. But that's okay. Whether it's mid-century art, first-edition books, or Bordeaux wines, all collectors have one thing in common: They don't buy everything they see. That goes for clothes and accessories too . . . learn the difference between impulse buying and thoughtful collecting. . . .

To have style, there must be an emotional and physical connection and passion to the clothes you buy and own. . . . [But] don't wait for an invitation to buy an evening dress. When you see something you love, buy it!

—Isaac Mizrahi in How to Have Style

said Mizrahi was "a big mover and shaker in the industry. He brought back a . . . fresh, casual elegance. He looked back to the movie stars, but he brought an American contemporary feel."

TRYING TO HEAL AND MOVE ON

Mizrahi told White that he had to consider changing his career focus from design to acting, screenwriting, and film production. But he was torn: "I never imagined my role as a designer diminishing and my role in filmmaking expanding. It's not what I dreamed of 12 years ago. As an artist, I feel there is something noble about fashion."

Mizrahi gave a long interview to Miles Socha of *Women's Wear Daily*. He tried to describe his plans: "Up to this point, my first commitment has been to fashion, but now I don't know. . . .

I will always have a great love of fashion. . . . I will always be a fashion designer, but I don't know what form it's going to take."

Socha asked Mizrahi if he was tired of designing. Mizrahi said he had been "more and more in love with it." He said that fashion "hits you right in the face with the moment" and that it was influencing the fine art world more than fine art was influencing fashion: "Now art is supposed to be so much about a reflection. Before it was a prediction. Now fashion is prediction, and art is a reflection." He seemed to be saying that both fine art and fashion can reflect the current state of the culture and point forward to what is coming as well. Each art form can play each role—reflector or predictor—at different times. They also influence each other.

After the Socha interview, the Mizrahi screen goes blank for two years. For the rest of 1998, all of 1999, and most of 2000, there are no major interviews on record and nothing of note on his Web site timeline. He disappeared from public view. He spent time in his own personal wasteland, recovering from the death blow to his business. No one but Mizrahi and his closest friends knows what he went through and how low his spirits sank. But he came back into public life in late 2000 with a full-throated roar.

LIFE IS A CABARET

A famous play and movie, *Cabaret* (a cabaret is a small nightclub with song, dance, and comedy acts), has a theme song that begins, "What good is sitting alone in your room?/Come hear the music play/Life is a cabaret." Mizrahi banished the prophets of doom from his business's closing by creating a cabaret act from his journal entries.

He had a number of friends in the theater business, and they helped him create the act. It opened off-Broadway in New York at the Greenwich House Theater on October 19, 2000. He was back in the limelight.

His show was titled *Les MIZrahi*. He sang, told stories, vented, and joked. He played himself, or at least some version of his most interesting self. He stood at an easel making sketches of dresses for one of his favorite actresses, Audrey Hepburn. He cut a coat from cloth and sewed it while talking about his days as a designer. He joked about things that had happened to him; humor had helped heal him. He even gave the audience Rice Krispies Treats.

And he sang. Mizrahi was onstage with the Ben Waltzer Trio when he sang several songs, including "When You're Smiling," "Baubles, Bangles, and Beads," and "Tea for Two." He had a simple and appealing singing voice that surprised many who knew him. The voice training he received years before at the High School of Performing Arts was put to good use, as was his lifelong love of music.

New York Times theater critic Ben Brantley wrote a review of *Les MIZrahi*: "It is hard not to root for Mr. Mizrahi. He still has a boyish anxiety and eagerness to please.... He is guaranteed a cult audience that will come for the inside digs at difficult divas and rival designers.... And oh yes, the clothes. They include an all-black Beat look a la Audrey Hepburn in *Funny Face*, a white-tie ensemble, a polka-dot lounging robe and a rhinestone-studded suit. He wears them well."

Brantley pointed out that playing oneself is not easy. At times, Mizrahi seemed nervous and uncomfortable. But he was at his best when he simply talked as if to friends at dinner. And when he told the audience that he needs love and he hopes they will give it to him, he showed how vulnerable he could be, how open to others.

If life was a cabaret, he had gotten out of his room and come to it. He had risked failure and succeeded in a form of entertainment that makes many demands of the performer. He was back.

LOVE WITHOUT BORDERS

Soon after his cabaret act opened, Mizrahi went to an animal shelter. He noticed one dog that was not as eager to be held as all the rest. That appealed to him. He says on his Web site that he thought, "This is perfect, he doesn't need me." He took the dog home and named it Harry.

After closing his company, Mizrahi disappeared for a couple of years. When he returned, he stayed away from fashion, choosing to perform an autobiographical show called *Les MIZrahi*. Mizrahi also adopted a dog, Harry, and the two quickly became best friends.

Harry is a beautiful, long-haired, red-gold golden retriever and border collie mix. The combination makes him very friendly, and he has become inseparable from Mizrahi. Friends soon noticed that Harry and his owner wore matching sweaters on cold days. Wherever Mizrahi was, Harry was close by. Harry turned into the neediest dog in the world, of course. Mizrahi wrote that Harry's neediness was the price of love: "And that was what was missing from my life: love without borders."

THE ISAAC MIZRAHI SHOW

The whole world was introduced to Harry when Mizrahi began hosting his own television talk show after his cabaret act ended. The Oxygen cable network launched *The Isaac Mizrahi Show* in September 2001, taking advantage of the obvious appeal to audiences he showed during his act. This was an extension of his creating, expressing, and selling his larger-than-life personality.

The weekly show was a half hour long and featured guests getting up off the interview couch and doing something with the host. Mizrahi told entertainment reporters, "I think talk is more for when you're doing something." So, for example, when guest Janeane Garofalo came on, she played Ping-Pong with Mizrahi. She brought her Labrador retrievers Kid and Dewey to play with Harry. In keeping with how spontaneous the show was, there were several "accidents" on the sets, since the dogs were so excited to see each other.

Kristin Davis, from the television program and movie *Sex and the City*, went on a shopping spree with Mizrahi. Rosie O'Donnell got advice on a haircut. Natalie Portman helped give Harry a bath. Mizrahi designed jeans for actress Selma Blair.

The television hosting led to other television appearances. In March 2002 he played himself in an episode of *Sex and the City*, in scenes with Sarah Jessica Parker and Candice Bergen.

During breaks from the taping of *The Isaac Mizrahi Show*, Mizrahi boiled down his old cabaret act and did a free-form performance at Joe's Pub in New York in October 2002. He noted on his Web site that "the most fulfilling night of my life was when I played Joe's Pub. . . . It dawned on me what I was supposed to be doing in my life, which is a kind of improvisatory [spontaneous] entertainment." He had conversations with audience members that were unscripted. If the audience sometimes seemed like a hungry beast that needed to be fed, well, he would feed it.

THE MIZRAHI PERSONALITY

The personality that Mizrahi was showing and selling onstage and on television has many features. As a gay man from New York in the fashion business, Mizrahi does have some verbal quirks that comedians like to use in their stock characters. Mizrahi uses "fabulous" to describe many things. His audience, no matter who they are, is referred to as "girls." His guests, friends, and even himself, are "darling."

Another part of his public personality is that he is neurotic, a word he often uses to describe himself. Neurotics are extreme worriers. They are different from most people because they worry about things most people never even think about. They are usually temperamental (sensitive and moody), anxious, and fussy. But some neurotics have the courage to stress their individuality and sensitivity to others. They often are less obedient to authority and less willing to follow others into bullying of any kind. Mizrahi is one of those temperamental neurotics that the world may need more of.

He often talks about his fascination with astrology and with psychics. He wrote a long article in the *New York Times* on February 23, 2003, that explored his interest in the otherworldly and his feeling that he and other designers may be conduits for other forces:

> Donna Karan was a guest critic at the Parsons School of Design when I attended some 20 years ago, and within 10 minutes of her critique we all knew she was a Libra with a Virgo ascendant. . . . Astrology, tarot cards, numerology, aura reading, past-life therapy—things that doctors and computer

analysts wouldn't dream of taking seriously—are as basic to fashion people as basic black.... A fashion designer makes his [or her] living predicting what people are going to be wearing, and for me it's a relief when someone else is doing a little soothsaying.

One of Mizrahi's best friends, Will McGreal, is a psychic. Mizrahi wrote in the *Times* article that McGreal both gives him readings and just hangs out with him, sometimes making it hard to tell what is just a passing comment and what is a prediction. But Mizrahi suspects that he and many fashion people are drawn to those who take their clients' lives very seriously and try to see what is hidden. "Collections are supposed to be light, airy spectacles. Fashion galas are meant to be fun. A reading with a psychic may be one way fashion folks have to vent all that serious stuff inside."

As his *New York Times* article shows, part of Mizrahi's personality is his sense of humor. One of his astrologers told him that he should wear diamonds because they would have a positive effect on his life. Mizrahi wrote: "I had a private chuckle over that, thinking diamonds would have a positive effect on anyone's life.... I never liked men in diamonds, but I'm having a change of heart ... somehow I'll find the one diamond ring a man can wear every day. If P Diddy can do it, I can, too." At a discussion about the future of fashion, Mizrahi was asked about celebrity fashion designers such as Lindsay Lohan and Nicole Richie. He replied, as reported by Christoper Muther of the *Boston Globe*, "After a while a girl who borrows dresses all the time just can't have style.... It's not a collection [when they show their lines], it's just 'Hold on, I need to take pictures tonight....' You wonder if these people actually go and buy something."

Perhaps Mizrahi's most notable personality feature is his boundless energy, his mania. Many people are familiar with the term manic-depressive, or bipolar, to describe people who have rapid mood swings from joy to depression. Mizrahi seems much more manic than depressive.

MIZRAHI MANIA

People in a manic phase of manic depression act in a certain way. They sleep little, are restless and alert, are very talkative, have racing thoughts, and exhibit extreme emotional responses. They can be intensely goal oriented if they have their mania under control.

Andy Behrman, in his memoir *Electroboy*, described his experience with his own mania: "Mania is about desperately seeking to live life at a more passionate level . . . trying to live a whole life in one day. . . . My manic mind teems with rapidly changing ideas and needs; my head is cluttered with vibrant colors, wild images . . . sharp details." He wrote that sounds are crystal clear, so much so that his eyelashes fluttering on the pillow sound like thunder. Behrman described how his mania makes him feel that life appears in front of him in vivid detail as if it were on an oversized movie screen. Colors are almost cartoonlike in their brightness. Mizrahi seems to share some of Behrman's experiences with mania. The designer responds to color and shapes in a very intense way.

Being manic is the opposite of being cool, according to Mizrahi. His Web site quotes him as saying, "As a performer I've learned you can't afford to pretend to be cool . . . unless you really are cool, which I guess I am not."

But mania, the strongly upbeat half of manic depression, does not exist without at least some downside. Mizrahi jokes that he is not bipolar but "tri-polar." He has three basic emotional states, even though mania is the one in which he chiefly makes a living. He says on his Web site, "I don't know what it is with me. . . . Every other night, I feel really great. Every second night, I feel completely overwhelmed with work. . . . Every third night, I'm so bored I'm sitting answering dumb email and playing computer bridge."

Many creative people use their manic phases to fuel their art: Poets John Keats, Sylvia Plath, and Walt Whitman, as well as writers Virginia Woolf and F. Scott Fitzgerald and artists Vincent van Gogh and Andy Warhol are only a few examples. Like many famous people, Mizrahi's manic phase is not out of control. And his depressive phases do not seem as deep or destructive as any of these poets, writers, and artists. He doesn't want to be the tortured artist, and he wills himself not to be one.

PURE CREATIVITY

Robert Epstein explored the creative personality in an article for *Psychology Today*. He noted that creativity is not mysterious and magical. It is often about the interaction of established behaviors and ideas.

Creative people are willing to feel frustration and confusion, to work through a situation or problem to a new solution. They do so by expanding possibilities. They draw on different fields and bring them together. Of course, creative people are responsive to their surroundings. But they often shift their attention to things most people don't notice. They select details and features they think are important, and then exaggerate them or simplify them, often to make an impression on an audience. Finally, creative people develop a way to capture their ideas, often using a journal or sketch pad.

Creativity comes in many sizes. A purely creative chef invents entirely new recipes, while a less creative one may come up with new variations on old recipes. A purely creative scientist may have one brilliant idea after another, as Albert Einstein did, while a less creative scientist may have one idea that she or he explores for the rest of her or his life.

Mizrahi has pure creativity. He has come up with entirely original looks year after year, not staying with the refinement of one theme. He does not do knock-offs (designs that imitate others), the way some designers do. The world has rarely seen some of his most creative work, done one at a time for his couture customers.

Epstein wrote that two enemies of creativity are distraction and disappointment. A painter who has to sell art that goes well with sofas and then give 50 percent of his money to an art dealer may get both distracted and disappointed. And a fashion designer who has to worry about business investors, advertising costs, low profits, and getting movie roles can also get distracted and disappointed. But somehow Mizrahi's creativity has overcome all of its enemies, including himself.

RIGHT ON TARGET

Mizrahi never got completely out of fashion design after his business closed in 1998. He still had a license for shoes that he designed, and he even had a few clients for custom-made dresses among the loyal, rich, and famous. He just didn't have a company to reach a large market or the time to devote to designing. Then, suddenly, he had one of the largest retail companies in the world in business with him.

No fashion reporters know exactly how long Mizrahi and executives at Target had been talking about working together. *Women's Wear Daily* suspects that it was as early as July 2002. His

After the debut of his talk show on the Oxygen network, Mizrahi's popularity skyrocketed and led to a partnership with retail giant Target. While the decision shocked many, he saw it as an opportunity to create designer clothing for everyone.

show on the Oxygen cable network was giving him a great deal of publicity, which could be natural advertising for the major retail chain. He was connecting with all kinds of women who watched his show. His charm was winning over many new possible customers he hadn't had before.

Women's Wear Daily announced the fashion bombshell in late February 2003: Target would launch an Isaac Mizrahi for Target collection. Senior vice president for Target Trish Adams told *Women's Wear Daily* that Mizrahi's personality was "a perfect match for Target." Mizrahi himself would be in at least some of the Target ads to come; 1,141 Target stores would carry the collection.

The announced theme was "swingy classics—trench coats, a denim circle skirt, a turtleneck sweater with wide stripes." He would design chic khaki pants, simple and beautiful white shirts, and colorful sweaters. Some of the pieces would be modeled by actress Candice Bergen and her daughter, Chloe Malle, in *Vogue*. At the same time, Mizrahi announced that he was launching a couture business, IM to Order. He was back in the fashion business, in a big way.

The new clothes began arriving at Target stores in August 2003. Soon he was on the road selling. He went to Chicago's Navy Pier, the Iowa State Fair, and many other places. One Target salesperson told a reporter that Mizrahi's clothes were "a great product that speaks for itself. It's not super trendy." Mizrahi's clothes would now be known in places like Grand Forks, North Dakota, not just New York and Hollywood.

AN EVENING AT THE RAINBOW ROOM

On Wednesday evening, September 3, 2003, Target hosted an upscale cocktail party at the famous Rainbow Room in New York's Rockefeller Center for the official opening of the Mizrahi collection. Reporter Robin Givhan wrote for the *Washington Post* that each plate of hors d'oeuvres probably cost more than a Mizrahi Target dress. The room was filled with urns containing pink roses and sounds from a jazz band.

Mizrahi was the guest of honor and obviously enjoyed the role. He greeted guests by telling them he just quit smoking and complaining that he was fat. Many reassured him he was not.

Givhan reported that the route to the Rainbow Room ran through an intimate boutique containing rows of suede jackets, cotton shirts, and nubby suits. She wrote: "What sets Mizrahi's collection apart is the price and the pink. The designer's signature color turns up in suede gloves, corduroy blazers, shirts, Mary Janes, and a multitude of linings. But the price is the draw."

Targeting Target

The Target Corporation is the nation's second-largest discount retailer (a store that features lower prices than other kinds of stores, such as specialty stores and department stores), after Walmart. Journalists like Laura Rowley, in her book *On Target: How the World's Hottest Retailer Hit a Bulls-Eye*, argue that it is Target's culture of placing importance on design and fashion that fueled its growth from humble origins.

In 1902, George Draper Dayton started a small business in Minneapolis, Minnesota—the Dayton Dry Goods Company (dry goods are clothing, textiles, cosmetics, needles, threads, and more). He was known to be honest (his ads were not misleading), his store was clean and stocked with quality goods at fair prices, and he had a fair returns policy. Business was good and grew slowly, and the store eventually became the Dayton Hudson Corporation after some acquisitions.

By the early 1960s, discount retailing was hot. But the discount stores were not—they featured harsh lighting, annoying music and selling over loudspeakers, cluttered aisles (often with clothes on the floor), and few signs. Some grandsons of George Draper Dayton decided to

Target didn't have a permanent store in New York, so the boutique in Rockefeller Center was left open for six weeks. *New York Times* reporter Ginia Bellafante wrote that the Rockefeller Center Target boutique had most of its clothes in sizes, 12, 14, and 16. She called it "reverse snobbishness." She noticed that the clothes were not especially trendy. Denim and skirts fit on the waist, not the hips. Blazers were cut fitted and long, "as they were in the old days, when women did not try to look like boys prematurely sent off to boarding school." She called Mizrahi a "populist," and said his clothes always had "embodied the glamour of moxie over money."

try something new, a discount store that paid attention to fashion and design. It also had wide aisles (so two shopping carts could pass each other easily), good lighting, no music or selling over the loudspeakers, contemporary signs, fast checkouts, and plenty of well-lit parking. They called their store Target, to make sure people knew it wasn't the same as their Dayton Hudson department stores and in the hopes they were hitting something that was needed.

By targeting not just low prices but upscale merchandise for good value, and by recognizing that all retail shopping is about both emotions and finances, Target was successful. The corporate culture believed in creative people, which led to a Design for All series of partnerships with designers. The first was Michael Graves, an architect who enjoyed doing designs of things smaller than buildings (his famous tea kettle has been featured in several museum shows). He was followed in the late 1990s and early years of the following decade by Mossimo Gianulli's leather blazers and capri pants and Liz Lange's maternity clothes. But Target didn't want just one designer to take over, as Martha Stewart had done for Kmart. The store itself is the brand.

Target has become part of American culture, including its pronunciation as *Tar-ZHAY* (a joke that still leads many to believe it is French owned). Many people do not know that Target operates two criminal forensics labs that grew out of its investigations of crime and fraud. The labs have worked with the Federal Bureau of Investigation and the Bureau of Alcohol, Tobacco, and Firearms and have developed many successful crime-fighting techniques and methods.

A DEMOCRATIC DESIGNER

On June 14, 2004, Mizrahi held a fashion show at Cipriani 42nd Street, located in a New York City landmark building near Grand Central Station. It was a restaurant and lounge with golden chandeliers and marble columns. The collection combined elements of his couture line, IM to Order, and his Target line. *New York Times* reporter Ruth La Ferla wrote that "it is a combination of class and mass that seems without precedent on a fashion runway." A $20,000 skirt embroidered with an intricate patchwork design was worn with a $14.99 Target stretch-cotton shirt.

The Isaac Mizrahi Show focused on Mizrahi's ability to connect with different kinds of people, but whenever there was a break in filming, he continued to pursue his other interests. The designer continued to perform a version of his old cabaret act at Joe's Pub in New York City.

Mizrahi told La Ferla, "This is just so democratic. My goal is that you won't always be able to tell the difference between what is Target and what is couture." His creative instincts had taken two different looks and combined them. He would often later call his theme for the Target collection "prestige for the masses," which he labeled "masstige."

Mizrahi said he lives his own life with the high and low, "in custom-made suits from England and polo shirts from Gap." His studio in Greenwich Village where IM to Order was now located was his couture headquarters, as well as the place where he worked on the Target collection. When he was asked if it was confusing to have a $30 sweater be mistaken for one priced at $300, Mizrahi said, "If it freaks people out now, it will turn them on a few months from now. I don't know what's more chic than a sable-lined raincoat worn with $25 penny loafers."

By late 2004, Mizrahi's Target line was selling extremely well. So he started to design housewares, including towels, sheets, dishes, and shower curtains. Then in October 2004, he appeared on the television show *The Apprentice*. The contestants were challenged by host Donald Trump to design a new line for Target.

Mizrahi's couture line was also selling well. His recovery from the devastating loss of his business in 1998 was now complete. Marisa Gardini, the chief executive officer at Isaac Mizrahi and now a close friend, told reporter Marc Karimzadeh from *Women's Wear Daily* that "everything is healthy, strong; it's [the business] growing and we are really happy." In addition, Mizrahi's entertainment career was about to take another big step.

5

Having Better Days

Mizrahi was now ready to integrate his fashion and entertainment worlds in one place. He supervised the building of a new headquarters on Tenth Avenue in New York. It became a sprawling, 18,500-square-foot (1,719-square-meter) space that was partly a design studio for his couture and Target designers, pattern makers, and seamstresses. But it was also a television studio for shooting shows.

The television studio had a square stage platform lit from underneath and room for a small audience. There were separate stages for the Ben Waltzer Band and for a high-tech kitchen for cooking segments. His mother told reporters that the space was "awesome. . . . It's so Isaac, but I didn't expect it to be so big."

THE NEW SHOW ON STYLE

His Oxygen cable network television show had lasted three seasons, and Mizrahi was now ready for an even bigger show, a full hour long, each day of the week. He began filming for his new talk-show program on the Style Network in 2005. He told *New York Times* reporter Lola Ogunnaike that he wanted spontaneity to be the key. He said: "On a lot of shows you can feel the guest is being set up [by interviewing before the show off camera, called pre-interviewing] to tell the cute story. I'm like, 'Let's not and say we did.'" He always loved being unscripted. Ted Harbert, president of Style and E! networks, told Ogunnaike that Mizrahi was "magic with people. People either want to hug him or laugh with him."

On December 5, 2005, *Isaac: Have a Better Day* premiered. His interviewing style was usually gentle, not probing for dirt. He didn't want celebrities' handlers and agents having anxiety attacks when their clients came on his show. And, as an astrology buff, he almost always asked his guests about their zodiac sign (he is a Libra with Virgo rising).

During the very first show, he told actress Keira Knightly that Jane Austen's *Pride and Prejudice* was his favorite novel, putting her at ease (he did, however, forget the plot). A few weeks later he had *The Sopranos* actor Steve Schirripa on the show and played bocce with him, telling him he loved the actor's square-toed shoes. He may not have been completely sincere, but he enjoyed bantering with his guests and almost always noticed what they were wearing.

Ogunnaike watched a show being taped and wrote: "His large hands flitter about like wayward kites when he speaks, and like any designer worth his weight in fabric, he is given to grand pronouncements. . . . Subtlety has never been his thing." *New York Times* television critic Virginia Heffernan wrote: "The fashion star still seems like an overgrown spoiled kid who was told he was a genius way too many times. . . . But when he's front and center, and getting all the attention he needs, there's something infectious about his self-delight."

TRIPPING ON THE RED CARPET

Perhaps nothing made Mizrahi more famous and infamous in the entertainment world than his time on the red carpet. He joined the E! Entertainment Television shows interviewing celebrities before the Golden Globes on January 16, 2006, and the Academy Awards on March 5, 2006.

His most notorious interview was with actress Scarlett Johansson just before the Golden Globes ceremony. She was wearing a stunning red Valentino gown with a plunging back, and he touched the dress under her chest as he asked what kind of support the dress had. She laughed but later said she was slightly uncomfortable. As a designer, Mizrahi was used to touching models and rearranging clothes, so he was shocked at the outpouring of criticism about his touching Johansson's chest. He also interviewed actresses Teri Hatcher and Eva Longoria, asking them personal questions about undergarments. Again, he was surprised at the reaction of the entertainment press, which felt he had gone too far.

Mizrahi told *USA Today*'s Pop Candy blog, "I just asked the questions that interested me and my producers. . . . The last thing I want to become is one of those talking heads where everything is satiny smooth and you know what the next question is going to be."

He was warned by his bosses at E! to be more respectful of the celebrities at the Academy Awards, held a few weeks after the Golden Globes. He told cohost Ryan Seacrest as they stood on the enormous red carpet leading to the Kodak Theater, "I'm going to be so good I'm going to have a halo by the end of the evening."

He behaved. He put actress Sandra Bullock at ease with easy questions and asked Dolly Parton about her earrings. He did ask *Crash* star Matt Dillon if his tuxedo was a rental, and Dillon played along and said it was. Mizrahi interviewed Jessica Alba and Keira Knightly, and then disappeared off the air well before the Oscar ceremony began.

The E! Entertainment News Network hired Mizrahi as a red carpet correspondent for the 2006 Golden Globe Awards. Although the designer and entertainer brought his usual energy and warmth to his coverage, many thought he was too forward and even inappropriate in his celebrity interviews. *Above,* Mizrahi interviews actress Anne Hathaway before the 2006 Golden Globes.

DESIGNING COSTUMES

Mizrahi has always enjoyed designing costumes for stage plays and operas. He created the costumes for the Broadway revival of *Barefoot in the Park*, starring Patrick Wilson and Amanda Peet. His Web site says that this is one of his favorite plays: "The period speaks to my childhood."

The original play, a romantic comedy by Neil Simon, opened on Broadway in October 1963 and ran for almost four years. It tells the story of a newlywed couple trying to adjust to each other and make a life in Midtown Manhattan, coping with a tiny apartment with no heat and strange neighbors. The revival opened in February 2006, and Mizrahi's costumes got more favorable reviews than the rest of the production.

In July 2006, Mizrahi's costumes for an opera about King Arthur were on display in London. Soon after, he worked with his friend Mark Morris on costumes for the opera *Orfeo ed Euridice* at the New York Metropolitan Opera.

ACCESSORIZING IN STYLE

When Mizrahi was in business in the 1990s, his company had designed and manufactured two main accessories, shoes and handbags. That had been difficult, given problems with suppliers and cutthroat competition. He told *Women's Wear Daily* reporter Jennifer Hirshlag, "When I was in business before, I tried to go into accessories, but we were doing it all in-house and it was such a huge job."

In early 2006, he tried a new approach. He licensed his name to two companies that made and sold shoes and handbags. He told Hirshlag: "I'm always designing shoes and bags, but they take on lives based on opportunities. . . . It's been this long, slow process of finding the right partners." That meant he could concentrate on helping design, but not have to worry about other business aspects.

The Los Angeles–based company Fashion House Inc. agreed to manufacture and distribute an Isaac Mizrahi line of both expensive shoes (costing more than $500) for upscale department and specialty stores, and more affordable shoes to be sold at Target and other discount stores. Mizrahi told *Women's Wear Daily*, "I always love the high and the low. I love that it's democratic . . . that a little cheap shoe could be as gorgeous as an expensive one."

The Accessory Network Group in New York agreed to manufacture and distribute Isaac Mizrahi handbags for both the high end ($395 to $795) and the lower end ($20). Abe Chehebar, chief executive officer at Accessory Network Group, told *Women's Wear Daily* that Mizrahi "can implement his designs and ideas for the designer level, as well as the mass level. There's a lot of cross-shopping going on now and [Mizrahi's] direction was visionary."

Mizrahi told *Women's Wear Daily* that consumer tastes needed variety. A diet of only pizza would bore someone, as would only a diet of expensive items like caviar and truffles. "It's the same with clothes and décor," he said. "Halston began to see the light, but he couldn't do it because society wasn't ready for it. It feels right to me now."

He also wanted to be able to coordinate accessories with each other and with clothes. "A woman thinks a lot about shoes and bags, as they work together. It's something I've always thought about and wanted to do." He told Hirshlag that accessories, not clothes, were the motor driving the fashion world in 2006. "In order to make yourself fashionable now, the first thing you think about are your bag, your clothes, your hairstyle."

SNAPSHOTS FROM 2007

Mizrahi's Web site timeline describes several scenes from 2007. In February, during a fashion show at Bryant Park for his fall 2007 collection, he waved to the crowd from a wheelchair. He had been in a car accident the week before, but he wasn't letting his injuries slow him down. He called the collection Frozen Spring and noted that this was the first time in three years that he had shown his designs during Fashion Week in New York.

In March 2007, he launched a collection of fabrics for home furnishings for Target. In May, he was back at Joe's Pub doing his cabaret act. He also went to Las Vegas for the first time and visited the Liberace Museum to enjoy the clothes and memorabilia from a show business legend. He met Celine Dion in Las Vegas and even ate at a Chili's restaurant for the first time. During that same month, he launched a bridal gown collection for Target.

When Mizrahi's contract with Target expired, he joined Liz Claiborne as the company's creative director. Because Liz Claiborne is known for creating stylish yet affordable work attire for women in corporate America, many believed Mizrahi would be a natural fit with the company.

In December, he appeared with Martha Stewart on her television show. They would soon launch a weekly call-in show on Sirius Radio called *Tell Me Everything*. He was also writing his book *How to Have Style*, which would be published in 2008. All in all, 2007 was just a typical manic year for a multimedia celebrity.

MOVING TO LIZ CLAIBORNE

Mizrahi's collection for Target had been a huge success, generating more than $300 million a year by the end of 2007. Sales had doubled every year since the launch in 2003. But his contract with Target was due to expire at the end of 2008, and like a great professional athlete, other teams wanted the designer. And so talks began behind the scenes, lasting for months.

On January 15, 2008, the fashion world was rocked by another Mizrahi bombshell. He was leaving Target at the end of 2008 to become the creative director for Liz Claiborne Inc. *Women's Wear Daily* reported that the deal was negotiated by an executive for partnered brands at Liz Claiborne, Dave McTague, who said: "Isaac is an amazing designer, but also an astute, successful, and innovative businessman. . . . His own core values as a designer—among them fit, color, comfort, style, and value—mesh perfectly with the philosophy under which this brand was founded." Liz Claiborne chief executive officer William McComb told *New York Times* writer Cathy Horyn: "There's magic in his shop. Part of what I felt we were buying into was a culture—a designer-led, irresistible culture."

Mizrahi told reporters in a prepared statement:

Liz Claiborne is an American fashion icon. Her clothes were not only beautiful, not only smart, they were revolutionary. She invented separates, and invented an entirely new category in the department store.

She made fashion friendly and accessible, and in doing so, she became every woman's best friend.

The Genius of Liz Claiborne

Anne Elisabeth Jane Claiborne was born on March 31, 1929, in Brussels, Belgium. Her parents were Americans abroad, her father an international banker. She spoke French before she spoke English, and she always seemed to say what was on her mind, even as a child. The family left Europe for New Orleans, Louisiana, when she was 10 (she was a descendant of a Louisiana governor). But she returned to Europe before finishing high school to study art and fashion design. She was fiercely independent.

At age 19, during a family trip to New York City, she told her parents, "I'm staying." Her father gave her $50 and wished her luck. She soon found work in the back rooms of Seventh Avenue as a model and design assistant.

New York City in the late 1940s was a special place at a special time. The city and country were well into a period of relative peace and prosperity after one of world war, economic depression, and horror. As Cathy Horyn describes in the *New York Times Style Magazine*, a sea of secretaries, shopgirls, and telephone operators flowed into the Empire State Building, Seventh Avenue, and Macy's in the morning and out at night. Liz Claiborne was one of them.

Clearly Mizrahi was being brought in to help rebuild Liz Claiborne's business and image. The company's main label had not been doing well for years, and Liz Claiborne herself had retired from the business in 1989 and had died in 2007. The company seemed to be a house divided, with the designers often losing out to the sales department in major decisions. A strong designer was needed.

Fashion expert Jennifer Black reported that the move to get Mizrahi would help slow down the loss of Liz Claiborne orders

At age 21, Claiborne won a design competition sponsored by *Harper's Bazaar* with her sketch for a woman's coat. Her career started to take off. She worked her way up the fashion corporate ladder for 25 years.

In the mid-1970s, her employer did not agree with her that a line of comfortable professional clothing for working women was needed. So, she resigned and, with the help of her husband, Arthur Ortenberg, started her own company in 1976, Liz Claiborne Inc.

Liz Claiborne Inc. concentrated on making practical clothes that were high quality, well made, comfortable, and affordable. Claiborne was a genius for insisting that millions of American working women needed their own look and for realizing they didn't have time to shop in several different departments: She wanted her clothes shown together, starting a revolution in retailing.

The clothes were instantly popular. And the company had perfect timing: It served an exploding market of woman graduating from high school and college in the 1970s and entering the working world in record numbers. Many women remember their first Claiborne outfit—a twill skirt needed for a job interview or a navy blazer to fit into corporate culture—as a rite of passage into the working world.

By 1986, Liz Claiborne Inc. had sales of $1.2 billion, making it one of only two companies on *Fortune* magazine's list of the largest 500 American industrial companies that was founded by a woman. Claiborne retired in 1989 but did not stop working: She started foundations devoted to both environmental conservation and helping end domestic violence and dating abuse. When she died in June 2007 at age 78, the fashion world knew that it had lost a legend.

from retailers once his influence was felt. Black said: "It's a great move for Liz Claiborne, and a huge loss for Target. . . . Isaac really understands this customer, and he has done the high-end and really done a great job targeting it to the mainstream."

The company's chief creative officer, Tim Gunn, was one of the hosts of the popular television show *Project Runway*, and now the company had two highly visible creative people on board. The fashion world waited to see how the two strong personalities would work with each other.

A NIGHT AT THE MUSEUM

Monday, May 5, 2008, was a night at the museum for Mizrahi. The Costume Institute at New York's Metropolitan Museum of Art gives an annual Party of the Year that attracts celebrities and many in the world of fashion—designers, editors, writers, models, and executives. Invitations to the event are coveted. The theme for the May 2008 party was "Superheroes: Fashion and Fantasy," in honor of a new exhibition on the first floor of the museum.

The exhibition explored the connection between superheroes and fashion. Both transform people and empower them. The cape, mask, and/or bodysuit of comic book figures like Batman, Superman, Wonder Woman, Catwoman, and Iron Man are part of their transformation into someone powerful. Their costumes identify them and symbolize their strength.

The party was on the opening night of the special exhibition. The hosts were actors George Clooney and Julia Roberts and editor Anna Wintour. The *Vogue* editor was dressed in a silver-sequined, padded, floor-length Chanel gown. She told *New York Times* reporter Eric Wilson that she was Storm, the X-Men character: "I control the weather." The weather was beautiful, and most of the 750 guests came early. The hosts greeted them, as Wilson described:

> "Hi, I'm Julia," Ms. Roberts said over and over, playing up the comic book theme in a silver sparkly dress by Giorgio Armani, who was also in the receiving line. "It does take extra powers to stay up late," Ms. Roberts said.
>
> Before dinner, which was held in the Temple of Dendur (redecorated with plexiglass crystals protruding from the water, surely just the way they do on Krypton), the assorted guests made their way through the exhibition. . . . Isaac Mizrahi walked by, ignoring the clothes as he looked at his own reflection in a mirror. "Isn't it lengthening?" he asked, before being distracted by a mannequin in a flight suit.

The guests could see Superman's cape with its red-and-yellow shield and Wonder Woman's American flag–based costume, among many other superheroic looks in the exhibition hall. Model Gisele Bündchen told Wilson, "I want to take that Wonder Woman costume down and wear it right now, but it probably would be too revealing." Her date for the evening, New England Patriots quarterback Tom Brady (now her husband), said, "I want her to wear the Wonder Woman outfit." Wonder Woman actress Lynda Carter, designers Donatella Versace, Vera Wang, and Gilles Mendel, and tennis player Venus Williams were only a few of the famous guests who knew that fashion and superheroes are a natural match.

A NEW REALITY SHOW

Project Runway is a television reality series hosted by supermodel Heidi Klum and featuring Tim Gunn as an advisor to young designers trying to win a competition for best design. The show, like most reality television shows, features real people in challenging situations. Young or unknown designers try to create beautiful and useful fashion within time and budget limits. Tim Gunn walks among them in a Parsons School workroom as they sketch, design, cut, sew, and fit their creations. He tells them to "Make it work." The drama, cattiness, talent, and stress displayed make for must-see television.

The Bravo cable channel lost the show to rival Lifetime Television after a legal battle with *Project Runway*'s owner, the Weinstein Company. Bravo needed a replacement and turned to Mizrahi. The result was *The Fashion Show*, which premiered on Bravo on May 7, 2009. The show features a competition between some 15 designers, and each show has two challenges, which vary. The season winner gets her or his designs sold in retail markets and a cash prize of $125,000.

The show runs on Mizrahi's wit but also his honesty, which could be all too real. In the first episode, Mizrahi told the young designers after their first show, "I sat at that fashion show a little embarrassed. And I thought to myself: If any of these people worked for me, they would be fired immediately."

New York Times television critic Alessandra Stanley reviewed *The Fashion Show* after it premiered and compared it unfavorably to *Project Runway*. "Mr. Mizrahi, who can be very funny as well as flamboyant, is mostly a scold here. Ms. Rowland [cohost Kelly Rowland, formerly of Destiny's Child] is not exactly nurturing, either." She found Mizrahi's motto of "Keep pluggin'" to be less than inspiring.

But Mizrahi's personality shone through, and the show attracted about one million viewers each week in its first season. Viewership increased almost every week, so it was renewed for a second season.

Hoping to compete with the highly successful *Project Runway,* the Bravo Network commissioned its own reality competition, *The Fashion Show.* Mizrahi brought his usual energy to the show, but he also became known for his honest criticisms of its contestants. *Above,* judges Fern Mallis (*left*) and Kelly Rowland (*center*) with Mizrahi during the show's first season.

THE JOY OF BLOGGING

Mizrahi began a video blog in 2009 and began sending tweets on April 20, 2009. He always shows what is on his mind. On August 17, 2009, he was worried that fashion was losing ground to home decor and food in what excited people. He suggested that everyone go shopping immediately.

On September 16, 2009, he told the camera on the blog site that his spring 2010 fashion show was the next day and he needed to get some positive energy. A few days later, he was on vacation after the exhausting show, enjoying warm fall weather in New York. He described shopping for peaches and tomatoes at a farm stand and trying to make a Martha Stewart recipe for tarts. He said there was "no joy in the peach" that year.

His October 7, 2009, video showed him backstage at a taping of *The Martha Stewart Show*. Harry was with him, and Mizrahi described his love for the nine-year-old dog. And on October 10, 2009, he said in his video blog that he once thought he understood fashion models, then stopped, but now was inspired by them again.

On November 5, 2009, he showed how excited he was about the New York Yankees winning the World Series. He is a big Yankees fan, especially when they win. He wanted a World Series ring, badly. He asked someone on his staff to look into getting him one.

One of his blogging themes is dieting and nutrition. He is almost always trying to lose weight, using portion control, exercise, stretching, the Atkins diet, Weight Watchers, caffeine, banning candy at fittings, and nervous energy to keep off the pounds. But his love of homemade ice cream, chocolate-covered almonds, and doughnuts will always be ready to derail his diets.

VERSATILE AND VISIBLE IN 2010

January 2010 took Mizrahi into several green rooms (studios for guests about to appear on shows), including the CNN green room waiting to go on a show with Anderson Cooper, and the Rachael Ray green room. His trips to various television shows have been

ELEMENTS OF STYLE

All through elementary and high school, Regan [a client of Miz-rahi's] wore a uniform of sorts. Her parochial school uniforms and hoodie-and-sweats in her college colors left her no opportunity to show off her artistic side. Now that she was entering the so-called real world, Regan wasn't sure how she should dress.

There's nothing wrong with having a uniform or a style that you wear every day. . . . But what you want is your own personal uniform that makes you stand out. . . . Regan's wardrobe colors of choice were a yawn. Brown—lots and lots of brown—along with blah teal blue, drab greens, and murky reds. Even her lipstick was brownish. . . . I wanted to see Regan wear gray, navy, and black with an occasional splash of red and oatmeal as accents. I told her she has to carefully consider each and every item she purchases. I want her to have fun when she shops yet remember that she's entering womanhood. Her clothes have to be more meaningful and versatile. She's at a turning point in life. It's time for her to cast off childhood and have fun as an adult.

—*Isaac Mizrahi in* How to Have Style

almost nonstop. His lifestyle collection show on the QVC Channel, *Isaac Mizrahi Live!*, features the designer promoting everything from striped sweaters to stylish and colorful handbags, from cheesecakes and cookies to sunglasses and fine china. Performing and selling are two sides of the same coin for him.

On January 28, 2010, he said on his Web site that he was delighted that First Lady Michelle Obama wore one of his dresses to the State of the Union Address the night before. The dress was described as an aubergine (dark purple, or eggplant-colored) silk-and-knit "elegant but also ready to work" gown with three-quarter length sleeves. The first lady is a fan of Mizrahi and his work, and he is a fan of her and her husband.

In early February 2010, his collection for the fall 2010 show still needed work. He described the process as fitting, meltdown, rethinking, refitting. The jewelry had arrived for the show, but the handbags had not. Last-minute calls were frantic. But he also said that he enjoys the design process now more than ever.

He said that he knows this is clothes, not brain surgery, and that relaxes him a little in the tense days before a show. But he also joked on his Web site that his favorite television show is *Grey's Anatomy* and he thinks he takes his job more seriously than the surgeons portrayed on the show.

On February 18, 2010, his models hit the blue-lit runway at Bryant Park in a spectacular show of his fall 2010 collection. The pulsing beat of music from the Bad Plus kept the energy high. Beautiful models in dresses and skirts glittering in green, red, and gray flowed down the catwalk. Mizrahi came running out at the end, smiling and waving his arms, looking relieved and joyful all at the same time. He had triumphed again.

6

The Mizrahi Effect

ashion is a cultural force, and Mizrahi is a force within fashion. And he is a force that is multiplied by his ability to communicate in so many ways in many media. What he communicates is important: Be colorful and filled with spirit, and be compassionate.

He, like fashion itself, plays a role in how people define themselves. His fashions have both accepted and rejected stylistic traditions, so he gives people, mostly girls and women, choices in how they present themselves to the world. Girls and women can choose to stand out or fit in.

Mizrahi told interviewer Laurie Simmons, "I don't like people to feel completely and totally described by the clothes they wear of mine. I want them to feel that they're describing themselves, and then what they found of mine is helping them do that."

The Brave New World of Fashion Communication

Fashion communication has many components: reporting, editing, photography, advertising, public relations and publicity, visual merchandising and store planning, special events planning, and more. But fashion communication, like all communication, is changing at the speed of light.

Fashion shows are no longer exclusive events that can't be seen by most until the garments hit stores months later. Many are streamed live on the Internet. As a result, trends are seen sooner and knock-offs start faster.

Web sites that collect information from other Web sites (aggregator sites) now let shoppers sift through styles and compare prices from dozens of online stores. Fashion designers have iPhone and iPad applications to help get their messages out faster and to more people. They have to spend much more on digital advertising.

Young bloggers have a loyal following and the attention of fashion companies, editors, and designers. Jane Aldridge (Sea of Shoes), Tavi Gevinson (Style Rookie), Karla Deras (Karla's Closet), and Scott Schuman (The Sartorialist) are only a few of hundreds who post images of themselves in their favorite styles. These new voices have front row seats at fashion shows and often travel the world in search of the new.

Jane Aldridge was interviewed by the Associated Press's Jamie Stengle. Aldridge lives in a small Texas town, far from New York and Los Angeles, and is passionate about fashion. Her Web site shows her modeling outfits she puts together—on one day, a peach-colored skirt and a gray cropped sweatshirt. She said, "It (living in a small town and being interested in fashion) sort of inspires you to create your own little world."

Web sites combining fashion, entertainment, and e-commerce will only get more common. Some people, however, will always need the in-store experience, and the traditional fashion show, to inspire them.

He knows that people try to express something with what they wear. It can be a simple or complicated message that can be read by some and not others.

Cathy Horyn wrote in the *New York Times Style Magazine* that some girls and women want to buy a dress on Friday, wear it on Saturday, and forget about it on Monday. But others want to make things last, to be smart with their money and time. Again, Mizrahi designs for both.

But the force that Mizrahi has on the culture, the Mizrahi effect, is applied both to fashion and to people's lives outside of fashion. The Mizrahi effect is powerful because it is communicated well and radiates out from the fashion world. He is the face of a whole industry and in some ways a whole city, a face that is on television, radio, and the Internet almost every day. And he is the face and voice of an entire personality type—colorful, caring, manic, passionate, compassionate, temperamental, fussy, and slightly neurotic.

If fashion itself communicates, then Mizrahi has himself become a force for communicating about fashion. He has contributed to the rise of a new face of fashion, the bloggers who have a style all their own.

SPORTY GLAMOUR

The Mizrahi effect is everywhere in the fashion world. He has pioneered and championed high-low fashion, the pairing of the expensive and the inexpensive. He has brought more democracy to fashion, blurring the lines between the exclusive and the mass market. His clothes are inclusive, reaching out to young and old, straight and curved, hip and uncool. And mostly they are colorful.

Mizrahi's influence on the fashion world is summarized with something Cathy Horyn calls his "sporty glamour." He combines two kinds of fashion, the comfortable/practical and the glamorous. "Sporty" apparel emphasizes comfort, ease of movement, and casual style. Sportswear is a classic American fashion style. The word *glamour* originally meant a magic spell that made the viewer

A model wears one of Mizrahi's creations from his Fall 2010 collection. When he was creating this collection for Mercedes-Benz Fashion Week, Mizrahi regularly posted online entries that gave readers insight into his process of designing the clothes and organizing the production.

see something that wasn't there. The word still implies something with mystery and illusion that entices people to desire it. Glamorous people, places, and things trigger everyone's imaginations and fantasies. Glamour may disappoint and mislead because it is not all people want it to be, but glamour, like appearance, is very real and very much a part of life. And even though glamour sometimes dissolves into glitz and glitter, something that many people want but which does not satisfy at all when they get it, many people take their chances when trying to be glamorous, at least some of the time.

Mizrahi wants to make glamour that does not disappoint. He wants to create garments with mystery and illusion but that allow people to become more attractive and desirable versions of themselves. He often succeeds.

And Mizrahi has said many times that good taste in fashion is important, but one's spirit in wearing fashion is more important. He told Diane Clehane that "style is knowing when not to have any."

A NEW YORK STATE OF MIND

Part of Mizrahi's colorful personality and his effect on the culture at large is his connection to New York City. Mizrahi loves the city and what it offers. What he loves, he told Laurie Simmons, is that he gets to choose so many things:

> You have selective privacy. You have selective ethnicity. Everything is your own choice. And that's different from Europe and that's different from Asia. . . . In Paris it used to feel like you were living in a museum . . . but here you have just everything. And you don't necessarily live for the moment; you live for hope, you live for the next, for what you're going to get, what you're going to say, what you're going to think.

Colorful can mean "filled with rich variety" and being "vividly distinctive." Mizrahi and the city he loves are colorful in every sense. He has lived and worked in many parts of the city: the Upper East Side, the Upper West Side, Soho, Tribeca, Chelsea, Midtown,

Brooklyn, and more. Each is colorful, varied, and distinctive. The city's vivid variety nourishes him.

His New York state of mind includes being, like the city itself, theatrical. He wants attention (except when he doesn't). He, like fashion itself and the city he loves, is in the world's face almost all the time. But being in someone's face can mean confronting them for their own good or making them feel better. Mizrahi does both. New Yorkers have been known to do that as well.

In 2009, he opened a new boutique at 23 East Sixty-seventh Street in Manhattan. He told reporters he wanted to be nearer "his ladies." The wealthier and older women of the famous Upper East Side of Manhattan have been one of his target audiences. But it was also a part of New York City that he loved even more as he matured.

Although Mizrahi has not created a signature look that has made so many designers famous, many argue that his trademark is his inclusive style. His willingness to make beautiful clothing both practical and accessible has pushed the fashion industry to open its doors to mass-market retailers. *Above,* Mizrahi's Fall 2010 collection.

PASSIONATE COMPASSION

The Mizrahi effect includes compassion in all of its forms. Despite its reputation as cutthroat, most members of the fashion industry and those around them don't want to see each other fail. Fashion writer Robin Givhan noted that models will often work for nothing or are willing to take clothes as payment if they believe in a designer. Even public relations companies have been known to represent fashion designers for some time for almost nothing if they believe in their work.

Restaurants often allow a designer space for a show for next to nothing. Galleries do the same. Friends often help out struggling designers in many ways, by giving money or labor or other kinds of support. Givhan wrote, "They [supporters of those in fashion] also believe in the magic of the fashion industry as a place where it is OK to be counterintuitive, adventurous, and even unreasonable. That's good for the imagination, good for the culture."

Mizrahi told Diane Clehane that he feels a strong empathy with the struggling young designers on *The Fashion Show*. "After almost every elimination, I feel like sobbing. It's very, very sad for me [to have people on the show fail]." His video blog often shows his compassion for those less fortunate. The tenderness and affection he feels for audience members are always on display. And the theme of his book *How to Have Style* is offering help to those in need of fashion but also support.

WHAT'S NEXT?

As of early 2010, Mizrahi was cohosting *The Fashion Show*, cohosting a radio show called *Tell Me Everything*, starring in QVC's *Isaac Mizrahi Live!*, designing clothes for his line, serving as the creative director at Liz Claiborne, blogging at his Web site, and still doing his cabaret act at Joe's Pub. What he does is beyond multitasking. But his colorful and compassionate personality demands variety.

He told Marie Speed in late 2009 that his next phase of life is "immersion in the entertainment business. I'm going to write a

Mizrahi's talents and exuberant personality have made him a unique figure in fashion and entertainment. His ability to reach the American public has opened up opportunities for him in television, radio, and the Internet.

movie some day. I'm going to direct a movie some day, well, more than one." He will direct an opera in St. Louis soon. He doesn't know if he will succeed at every new venture. But he also said, "If you feel something in your heart, then you have nothing to worry about." What he has felt in his heart has guided him well.

Despite his ups and downs in business, he is first and foremost in love with designing, and more in love with designing than with fashion itself. Design is a set of guiding principles that allow him to make and appreciate beautiful and useful things. Fashion is more temporary, what is in style now and in the immediate future. No matter what he does next, it will involve designing in some way, and solving design problems. And he will believe in what he is doing, no matter whether it is designing a dress, baking a cookie, interviewing a celebrity, directing an actor, or having fun with an audience.

BRAVE SPIRIT

Part of Mizrahi's effect on the culture, his legacy, is his brave exuber-
ance that allows him to be himself and defy expectations. He does
what he has to, wants to, and needs to do, not what others expect
him to do. Many in the fashion world thought that after he had to
close his business in 1998, he would retreat into designing only couture for a few customers. He defied that expectation when he went
to work with Target, a venture he calls the most successful of his life.

His bravery includes his ability to jump into life. He rein-
vented himself as an entertainer after his business closed. But he
also never quit designing, his true love.

Bravery is doing the right thing. He told Marie Speed in the
interview for *Success* magazine, "The great lesson I've learned over

---

ELEMENTS OF STYLE

*[Ask yourself]: "How do you want to look and be remembered? Who
are you dressing for? Who are you trying to relate to when you put
yourself together? What do you want to say about yourself? How do
you see yourself? Who are you?"*

*[One of his clients, Manning Fairey, answered]: "I tend to
wear what's easy and inexpensive . . . I would be thrilled to find
my signature style and break out of the pack . . . I want to be fresh,
original, honest, and wholesome."*

*[Mizrahi's advice]: Wear all one color on top (for instance,
red) and another (navy) on the bottom, allowing the eye to travel up
and down smoothly. . . . Go to high-end stores and try on a bazil-
lion things by your favorite designers just to know what size you
are in that brand. . . . Then, on eBay, search by designer, not by
category. . . . As you look for your heart's desire, note which sellers
carry your faves. Build a relationship with those designers.*

—*Isaac Mizrahi in* How to Have Style

the years is . . . do what you want—don't let anyone tell you to do a version of what you want. Do exactly what you want, then wait it out." He tells people to listen to themselves first. Mizrahi told Diane Clehane, "Do exactly what you think is right, and you'll find your moment and your audience."

He also told Clehane, "For me, there's nothing in life but bravery. There's nothing in life but looking at the thing you're most afraid of and doing it." Conquering his fears took all he had, but it has given him fame. He has made it after all.

Chronology

1961	OCTOBER 14 Isaac Mizrahi is born to Sarah and Zeke Mizrahi in Brooklyn, New York. He is the youngest of three children and the only boy.
1966	Starts school at Yeshiva of Flatbush in Brooklyn in September.
1974	Begins attending High School of Performing Arts in Manhattan in September. Has bar mitzvah in October.
1978	Forms his first fashion design company, IS New York, with Sarah Haddad.

TIMELINE

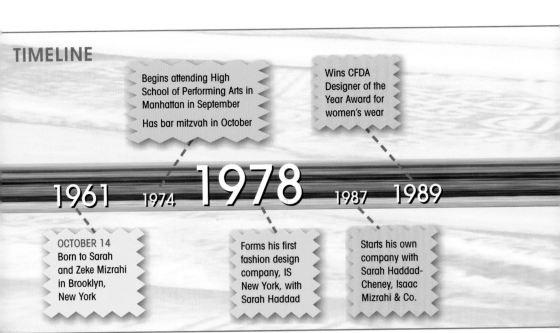

1961
OCTOBER 14 Born to Sarah and Zeke Mizrahi in Brooklyn, New York

1974
Begins attending High School of Performing Arts in Manhattan in September

Has bar mitzvah in October

1978
Forms his first fashion design company, IS New York, with Sarah Haddad

1987
Starts his own company with Sarah Haddad-Cheney, Isaac Mizrahi & Co.

1989
Wins CFDA Designer of the Year Award for women's wear

1979	Graduates from High School of Performing Arts in June. Begins attending Parsons School of Design full-time in September.
1982	Named one of eight Outstanding Student Designers at Parsons in April.
1983	Graduates from Parsons and immediately begins working full-time for Perry Ellis International.
1985	Hired by Jeffrey Banks Ltd. to help start a women's wear line.
1986	Hired by Calvin Klein.
1987	Starts his own company with Sarah Haddad-Cheney, Isaac Mizrahi & Co.
1988	APRIL First major show.

NOVEMBER Wins CFDA Perry Ellis Award for Emerging Talent. |

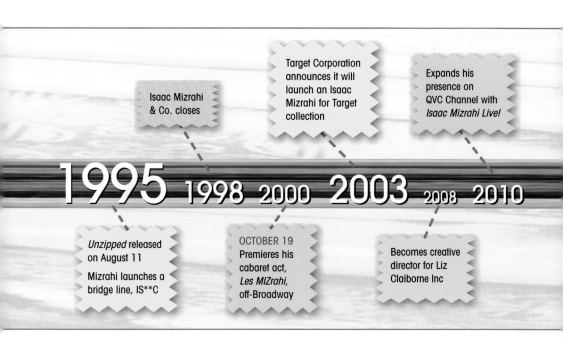

Isaac Mizrahi & Co. closes

Target Corporation announces it will launch an Isaac Mizrahi for Target collection

Expands his presence on QVC Channel with *Isaac Mizrahi Live!*

1995 1998 2000 **2003** 2008 2010

Unzipped released on August 11

Mizrahi launches a bridge line, IS**C

OCTOBER 19 Premieres his cabaret act, *Les MIZrahi,* off-Broadway

Becomes creative director for Liz Claiborne Inc

1989	Wins CFDA Designer of the Year Award for women's wear.
1991	Wins second CFDA Designer of the Year Award for women's wear.
1992	Chanel Inc. invests heavily in Isaac Mizrahi & Co.
1994	Famous fall collection show at Bryant Park on April 12; filmed by *Unzipped* staff.
1995	AUGUST 11 *Unzipped* is released and becomes a hit. Launches a bridge line, IS**C, to reach less expensive markets.
1998	Chanel Inc. withdraws investment; Isaac Mizrahi & Co. closes.
2000	Premieres his cabaret act, *Les MIZrahi*, off-Broadway on October 19.
2001	*The Isaac Mizrahi Show* premieres on the Oxygen cable network in September.
2002	Performs at Joe's Pub.
2003	Target Corporation announces it will launch an Isaac Mizrahi for Target collection in the fall. Mizrahi announces he will also head IM to Order, a couture company.
2005	*Isaac: Have a Better Day* premieres on the Style Network, December 5.
2006	Joins E! Entertainment Television red carpet team for Golden Globe and Academy Awards shows.
2008	Becomes creative director for Liz Claiborne Inc. *How to Have Style* is published.
2009	*The Fashion Show* premieres on the Bravo cable channel on May 7. Lifestyle collection show *Isaac Mizrahi Live!* premieres in December.
2010	Expands his presence on QVC Channel with *Isaac Mizrahi Live!*

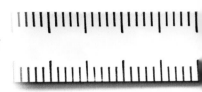

Glossary

accessory   Any item that is used to enhance or highlight wearing apparel. For example, handbags, jewelry, belts, gloves, and hats are all accessories. Some consider shoes accessories as well.

apparel   Clothes, garments, or anything worn that is not a shoe or accessory.

boatneck   Garment design with wide neckline, usually cut from shoulder to shoulder. Originally designed for sailors, who needed to get out of wet clothes quickly and easily.

bridge line   A collection or price classification that is priced between the two ready-to-wear categories of designer collections and mass-market collections. Bridge line apparel is made with fewer details and less expensive fabric than designer clothes.

capri pants   Women's pants that end near the midcalf.

casual wear   Apparel that emphasizes comfort and personal expression over formality.

catwalk   A narrow, usually elevated platform used by models to display clothing and accessories. Also called a runway.

chiffon pants   Usually loose-fitting, wide-leg women's pants made of sheer fabric such as silk, nylon, or rayon.

circle skirt   Cone-shaped garment worn from the waist having a bottom diameter wider than fitted skirts.

Council of Fashion Designers of America   Abbreviated as CFDA, the largest organization representing the fashion industry.

fashion blogs   Web sites created by people who have an interest in fashion design, celebrity fashions, and/or style in general.

fashion design   The art and craft of creating the form and texture of wearing apparel and accessories.

fashion forward   Representing the newest trends and styles.

fashion season   The period of time during which fashion products are sold. Traditionally, there are two main seasons, spring (including summer) and fall (including winter). But designers recognize subseasons as well, including holiday and resort.

fashion show   An event to showcase a designer's upcoming line of fashion products, usually either with models on a catwalk or in a staged setting.

haute couture   Customized and unique handmade garments made and sold or given to private customers or other exclusive clients.

knock-off   Fashion products copied from more expensive items and usually made with less expensive components and sold at a lower price than the original.

mannequin   Usually a life-size representation of the human body for fitting and displaying garments. Also called a dummy.

ready-to-wear   Apparel that is mass-produced in standard sizes. Two kinds of ready-to-wear garments are designer collections (more expensive) and mass-market collections (less expensive). Also called *prêt-à-porter* (from French).

secondary line   See *bridge line.*

Seventh Avenue   New York City's garment district.

shirtdress   A dress with details from a man's shirt, usually a collar, button front, and cuffed sleeves.

sportswear   Clothes worn for casual outdoor use or for sporting activities such as jogging, tennis, golf, and boating.

style   As related to fashion, the appearance of fashion products, expressing certain forms, price levels, and/or traditions.

tartan   Textile pattern with stripes of varying width and color crossed at right angles on a background; plaid.

textile   Fabric or cloth made of natural (such as cotton or wool) or synthetic (such as polyester) fibers, used for wearing apparel, linens, bedding, drapery, upholstery, and more.

Women's Wear Daily   Newspaper published each working day by Fairchild Publications. It is the fashion industry's most prestigious and reliable source of information on styles, trends, business dealings, laws, and people in the fashion industry. Often called "the fashion bible."

Bibliography

Behrman, Andy. *Electroboy: A Memoir of Mania*. New York: Random House, 2002.

Bellafante, Ginia. "In Mizrahiland at Target Stores, A-Lines and Suedes." *New York Times* (September 14, 2003).

Brantley, Ben. "First Presenting Clothes, Now Himself." *New York Times* (October 20, 2000).

Clehane, Diane. "So What Do You Do, Isaac Mizrahi?" Mediabistro.com. Available online. URL: http://mediabistro.com.

Epstein, Robert. "Capturing Creativity," *Psychology Today* (July 1996).

Foley, Bridget. "Isaac Mizrahi, Setting Out for Stardom." *Women's Wear Daily* (April 18, 1988).

———. "Isaac Mizrahi on Kilts, Celts, Fame." *Women's Wear Daily* (May 2, 1989).

———. "Isaac Mizrahi: His American Way." *Women's Wear Daily* (July 30, 1990).

———. "Isaac Unveiled." *Women's Wear Daily* (August 3, 1995).

———. "The Downfall of the House of Mizrahi." *Washington Post* (October 3, 1998).

———. "Talking Shop with Isaac." *Women's Wear Daily* (November 4, 2009).

Givhan, Robin. "Isaac Mizrahi Zips It Up for Target." *Washington Post* (September 5, 2003).

Heffernan, Virginia. "When Everyone's Fabulous, Especially Our Genial Host." *New York Times* (December 21, 2005).

Hochswender, Woody. "Fashion: Patterns; New Presence for Mizrahi." *New York Times* (February 14, 1989).

Horyn, Cathy. "Isaac Mizrahi Soared to the Top. So Why Aren't His Clothes Selling?" *Washington Post* (November 1, 1994).

———. "Can Liz Claiborne Get Its Groove Back?" *New York Times Style Magazine* (Fall 2008).

La Ferla, Ruth. "Isaac Mizrahi: Envying Roisterous Lives." *New York Times* (November 30, 1997).

Maslin, Janet. "A Madcap Maestro of Haute Couture." *New York Times* (August 4, 1995).

Mizrahi, Isaac. "Why We Love Fashion? It's Prescient." *New York Times* (February 23, 2003).

———. *How to Have Style.* New York: Gotham Books, 2008.

Morris, Bernadine. "Reviews: Fireworks and the Finale." *New York Times* (April 14, 1994).

Muther, Christopher. "Not Everyone's a Designer." *Boston Globe* (October 29, 2009).

Neuman, Joanna. "From Ghetto to Glamour: How Jews Re-designed the Fashion Business," Jewish Virtual Library. Available online. URL: http://www.jewishvirtuallibrary.org.

Ogunnaike, Lola. "On 'Isaac,' Food Tips and Stars, but Fashion Is King." *New York Times* (November 27, 2005).

Rowley, Laura. *On Target: How the World's Hottest Retailer Hit a Bulls-Eye.* Hoboken, N.J.: John Wiley and Sons, 2004.

Simmons, Laurie. "Isaac Mizrahi," *Index.* Available online. URL: http://www.indexmagazine.com.

Socha, Miles. "Isaac Mizrahi Shuts Down." *Women's Wear Daily* (October 2, 1998).

Speed, Marie. "Isaac Mizrahi: Following His Heart and Vision." *Success* (November 3, 2009).

Spindler, Amy. "Isaac Mizrahi Plays Himself." *New York Times* (September 27, 1994).

———. "A Designer Puts on a Show, a Friend Puts on a New Hat." *New York Times* (July 30, 1995).

Stanley, Alessandra. "Contestants Are Sewing, but the Hosts Are Cutting." *New York Times* (May 7, 2009).

Stebbins, Meredith. "Isaac Mizrahi's Walk in the Park." *Vanity Fair* (February 19, 2010).

Stengle, Jamie. "Online and Into Style." Associated Press (March 31, 2010).

White, Constance. "Mizrahi, Designer Most Likely to Succeed, Doesn't." *New York Times* (October 2, 1998).

Wilson, Eric. "Stars and Superheroes Sparkle at Museum Gala." *New York Times* (May 6, 2008).

Further Resources

Adato, Allison, and Fannie Weinstein. "A Second Act." *People* (August 18, 2003).

Beker, Jeanne. *Passion for Fashion: Careers in Style.* Plattsburgh, N.Y.: Tundra Books, 2008.

Breward, Christopher. *Fashion.* New York: Oxford University Press, 2003.

Grandon, Adrian, and Tracy Fitzgerald. *200 Projects to Get You into Fashion Design.* Hauppauge, N.Y.: Barron's Educational Series, 2009.

Hutton, Lauren. "Unzipped." *Entertainment Weekly* (March 8, 1996).

Kendall, Elizabeth. *The Autobiography of a Wardrobe.* New York: Pantheon Books, 2008.

Mizrahi, Isaac. *Isaac Mizrahi Presents the Adventures of Sandee, the Supermodel.* New York: Simon & Schuster, 1997.

Travers-Spencer, Simon, and Zarida Zaman. *The Fashion Designer's Directory of Shape and Style.* Hauppauge, N.Y.: Barron's Educational Series, 2008.

Udale, Jenny, and Richard Sorger. *The Fundamentals of Fashion Design.* Lausanne, Switzerland: AVA Publishing, 2006.

WEB SITES

Fashionista. Discusses interesting trends.
http://www.fashionista.com

Isaac Mizrahi. The designer's official Web site.
http://www.isaacmizrahiny.com

The Sartorialist. Interesting takes on fashionable people.
http://www.thesartorialist.blogspot.com

The Style Rookie. Fashion and style tips, insights, and reviews.
http://www.thestylerookie.com

Picture Credits

Index

About the Author

CLIFFORD W. MILLS is an adjunct faculty member at Columbia College, an editor, and a writer who specializes in biographies of world and cultural leaders as well as sports figures. He lives in Jacksonville, Florida.